GARDEN SHRUBS

| JANUARY | FEBRUARY | MARCH | APRIL | MAY | JUNE | JULY | AUGUST | SEPTEMBER | OCTOBER | NOVEMBER | DECEMBER |

A L L Y E A R R O U N D

Christopher Fairweather

PHOTOGRAPHS BY
Robin Fletcher
· AND ·
Christopher Fairweather

BLANDFORD PRESS
POOLE · NEW YORK · SYDNEY

*First published in the U.K. 1986 by Blandford Press,
Link House, West Street, Poole, Dorset BH15 1LL*

Copyright © 1986 Christopher Fairweather

*Distributed in the United States by
Sterling Publishing Co. Inc., 2 Park Avenue, New
York, N.Y. 10016.*

*Distributed in Australia by Capricorn Link
(Australia) Pty Ltd, PO Box 665, Lane Cove,
NSW 2066*

British Library Cataloguing in Publication Data

Fairweather, Christopher
  Garden shrubs the year round.
  1. Shrubs
  I. Title II. Fletcher, Robin
  635.9'76   SB435

ISBN 0 7137 1383 6

*Typeset by Megaron Typesetting, Bournemouth,
Dorset*

Printed in Spain by Graficromo, S.A.

GARDEN SHRUBS

ALL YEAR ROUND

JANUARY FEBRUARY MARCH APRIL MAY JUNE JULY AUGUST SEPTEMBER OCTOBER NOVEMBER DECEMBER

Contents

Introduction

Shrubs usually supply the main three-dimensional structure of a garden. Perhaps a few trees may provide high features, and of course herbaceous elements are very generally used to fill the intervals with changing effects of leaf and colour. Still, the formal arrangement consists mainly of the shrubs, and when people speak of 'the character of a garden', these are bound to comprise a vital ingredient.

Shrubs are a long-lasting and virtually permanent part of the garden scene. Once they reach a mature state, their physical form in terms of size and shape and habit of growth makes itself felt at all times of the year. Meanwhile their foliage changes from season to season – to a greater or lesser extent according to the characteristics of each particular evergreen or deciduous shrub.

The size and shape and density of the leaves, their light or dark tone, their actual colour, their shiny or matt surfaces, the textural effects produced by the way they are presented on the shrub and the appearance of flower among the leaves: all these details contribute to the visual delight a particular shrub can offer in a certain position in the garden and in proximity to other plants or features.

It is very easy to underestimate the importance of the foliage characteristics of a shrub to the effectiveness of its contribution to a scheme of garden design. Likewise, it is easy to get carried away with enthusiasm for flowering effects. Blossom, however lovely, is liable to be short-lived, and the garden wants to remain interesting at all times. So, to get the best out of garden shrubs all the year round, foliage may be regarded as the more important factor.

Flowering certainly has great importance. It is the most spectacular effect that most plants have to offer. The variety of colours, patterns and scent is fascinating and wonderful. Indeed the reproductive characteristics of the plant are such a distinctive factor that they provide the basis on which plants are botanically classified. Clearly this is a matter of the highest importance. Yet a garden that was set out solely on considerations of, say, the petal colours of the flowers produced, would almost certainly fail as a design. The sizes and shapes and habits of growth would be unco-ordinated, the leaves of one shrub would look silly or dull next to another; even the flowers could look wrong in character next to one another, or appear at the wrong time of year for the intended effect. For example, a pink shrub rose and a pink rhododendron would not associate well together. Their foliage is unsympathetic, they require quite different exposure, they fail to match in scale and their leaf structures have nothing in common.

Flowering is best thought of as a way of drawing special attention to the part of the garden where the blooming plant is situated. On these lines, seeing that there is no time of year when some shrub mentioned in this book is not in blossom, it is possible for every season to have at least some corner of the garden seen at its best.

The purpose of this introduction, and one of the special purposes of this book, is to draw attention to this way of considering the amazing resources of shrub plants now available through nurseries and garden centres. We can really enjoy them all the year round. Likewise for the enthusiast in shrub propagation, there is no season when some aspect of this activity cannot be pursued. Cuttings of different types can be taken at their appropriate season, and then require various sorts of further attention in a complete calendar of activity. Both these fascinating sides of the all-season interest of shrubs, as a category of plants, are taken together to form the subject of a book which I hope will be found useful and stimulating by readers of all levels of interest and expertise in this subject.

Part I
CULTIVATION

Choosing Shrubs for your Garden

Before you rush out to the nearest supplier to buy any shrubs, there are several important factors to be considered. If your garden is completely new, you will need to design its features carefully before deciding what to plant, and if it is established you will need to choose suitable types of shrub for the positions you wish to plant them in. The type of soil you have is also very significant when it comes to choosing the right plants.

Garden Design

Firstly, it is advisable to make a plan: this need not be anything elaborate, but spend time measuring out your garden and draw this out on a plain sheet of paper. Mark any existing features such as trees, hedges, paths or steps. Also, mark the aspect of your garden with a clear arrow pointing north, as this will enable you to pinpoint the sheltered corners. It is likely that you will need a fairly large section devoted to lawn, and possibly a smaller area could be paved. Do you require a vegetable garden? This should be planned, with perhaps the addition of a hedge or screen to hide it from the rest of your garden. Finally, when you have included all these features, you will come to the all-important shrub borders. Considering the final design, my advice is to keep it simple. For the smaller garden formal straight lines are not usually pleasing; instead try to make gentle flowing curves which are easy on the eye. Think of making a focal point and consider planting a few trees to give height.

The Soil

Next take a close look at the ingredient that ensures success or failure – the soil. Firstly, find out if it is acid or alkaline. An acid soil will allow you to grow almost anything, including all the glorious rhododendrons, azaleas and camellias, as well as a range of heathers.

If, on the other hand, you have an alkaline soil (containing lime), this will still allow you to grow a very wide and exciting range of shrubs (in some cases with greater success than an acid soil), but sadly this excludes all the ericaceous subjects. The easiest way to check the acid/alkaline level of your soil is to buy one of the simple testing kits from your local garden shop or centre: a small quantity of soil mixed in with the liquid will give a quick colour reading showing the pH (acidity) level.

The best type of soil is a well-drained fibrous loam. Unfortunately, it is rare that the soil is perfect and often we inherit either heavy clay, light sandy soil or a mixture of sand and gravel. The really heavy soil with a high clay content tends to become wet and sticky in winter, baking hard like concrete in summer. To achieve a workable tilth try to dig the heavy soils during late autumn to early winter, leave the ground rough allowing frost, wind and rain to play its part, and by spring the weather should have produced a good friable texture.

This is the moment to add plenty of humus in the form of moss peat, leaf mould or spent hops – producing a good growing medium which will suit most shrubs. Light sandy soils have a tendency to dry out during the summer months, so again plenty of humus should be added to retain all possible moisture. Mulching with peat, leaf mould or bracken will also be very beneficial.

Deciding on Suitable Shrubs

The following points should be borne in mind when making a selection of shrubs for a new garden, or indeed for use in an established garden when the existing shrubs should be complemented by the new additions.

1 Select a range of shrubs that will give interest throughout the year. This means that flowering time must be considered, as well as a selection of evergreen with interesting or bright foliage. Bright-coloured stems and interesting bark can add considerably to colour in the winter. Add in a few shrubs that are scented or have nice aromatic leaves.

2 Are you trying to screen anything? A selection of evergreens at the back of a border can act as an informal hedge and make a pleasant background.

3 Check carefully the ultimate size and spread of the plants you plan to include. When you plant, allow plenty of space – there may appear to be too much bare earth showing, but have patience, as many shrubs grow surprisingly fast and require plenty of space if they are to give of their best. If you are concerned about the bare earth, fill it in with something that can be easily transplanted, such as herbaceous plants or seasonal bedding. When the shrubs expand these can be moved.

4 Give thought to the scale of your garden; if it is quite small the last thing you require is a giant shrub growing up to 20 ft (6 m) high and wide that will dominate everything. Also, it is fairly obvious when planting that all tall-growing plants should be at the back and low-growing ground-cover types in front.

5 Finally, consider the various aspects of your garden. Look for the sheltered corners where the more delicate subjects can be planted.

Warm south or west facing walls are best for tender plants; the east can be cold and exposed to bitter winter winds, therefore plant your hardy subjects there. North, again, can be cold and lacking sun, but will suit many shrubs that are damaged by the combination of early morning sun and frost such as the spring-flowering camellias.

What to look for when you buy

The majority of shrubs sold now are 'container grown', which means that throughout their life they have been grown in a pot. Obviously the great advantage of this is that planting can, in theory, be carried out twelve months of the year if the weather is favourable. Nevertheless, avoid periods when frost and cold winds are expected, as well as very dry summer months – otherwise any time is planting time.

When you purchase your shrubs remember that these plants will be with you for many years, therefore do not necessarily look for instant success, choosing small plants covered in flower buds. Look for plants that will develop into well-shaped specimens. So often I have seen small 12 – 15 in (20 – 45 cm) high rhododendrons covered in buds – certainly you may get a marvellous spring display but the plant will be so weak after this great effort that you may get no growth.

Avoid naturally any plant that shows any sign of disease; look for well-branched, healthy specimens in a good-sized pot which allows for well-developed roots. Follow carefully the planting instructions which follow and you should have many years of trouble-free colour and enjoyment with the minimum of upkeep.

Ground Preparation

This operation is of course vital for the future success of your shrubs, the majority of which should spend many years growing and flowering in your garden. Preparation and care at planting time may well make all the difference between success and failure. So often people say that they bought a shrub, planted it in the garden and it died. In many cases this is due to inadequate preparation. Perhaps you have a brand new garden or plan to extend a shrub border; here are a few points to consider.

1   Make sure that the site you choose is well drained. Few shrubs will thrive if they are sitting in very wet soil for months on end. Excess water should be led away in land drains, and this must be done before cultivation and planting. If you notice moss growing on the soil this is definitely a sign of bad drainage; rushes are even worse! Badly drained soil excludes all the air which prevents the development of healthy roots.

2   Before planting take all possible steps to remove any perennial weeds, especially the pernicious couch and, even worse, bindweed and ground elder. It is advisable to delay any planting until the ground is totally clean. Once you have planted your shrubs these wretched weeds will be all among the roots and become virtually impossible to eradicate. Weedkillers (see p. 21) can certainly be useful aids, but rarely will they clean up an established shrub border badly infected with perennial weed.

3   In a new garden look out for builders' rubble, because they can be very clever at burying all their old bricks, slates and subsoil from the foundations. When this rubble is covered over with an inch or two of good top soil, all looks well until you try pushing in a fork or spade to do some planting. However tedious, remove this rubbish and replace with top soil.

4   Quite a few shrubs will not tolerate any lime in the soil, i.e. an alkaline soil. If you are uncertain about the acidity or alkalinity (pH) of your soil, various firms will undertake a soil analysis, or you can do it yourself with one of the simple testing kits available from garden centres and shops. For rhododendrons and azaleas, a slightly acid soil with a pH of about 6 is ideal.

Planting

It is a good idea to wait until there are a number of shrubs to go in and then have a definite planting session. Fill the wheelbarrow with a quantity of coarse sphagnum peat mixed with sharp sand, with a quantity of well-rotted manure or compost added. A small amount of fertiliser such as growmore or bone meal can be added, although sometimes it is better to give a light feed once the plants are established and the roots are working well.

When to plant

Today more and more of the shrubs we buy are growing in pots, therefore it is fair to say that any time is planting time. Nevertheless, there are definitely times of the year when growing conditions are at their best, and your shrubs have more chance of success. Traditionally the planting time has been autumn, given the cool damp weather, and this is an excellent time. Planting through the winter months depends to a large extent on the weather; if it is very cold or very wet it is best to delay. Start again as spring begins and carry on well into early summer avoiding the hot dry months.

How to Plant

Whether it is for a shrub with bare roots or one pot grown with a rootball, it is advisable to take out a planting hole about twice the required size. With a fork break up the soil at the base, as this helps the roots to make their way down and improves drainage. I then mix some of my special planting brew of equal parts of peat and sharp sand and incorporate a good shovelful with the soil taken from the planting hole. Replace about half of this peat/sand/soil mix back into the hole; this provides a good base for the new shrub to send down roots. Place the shrub into the planting hole, making sure not to plant it too deep. With a spade or trowel spread the remainder of the soil around the roots, gently shaking the plant to ensure that it settles in well. Finally, firm gently with your foot and your new shrub should grow away without any trouble.

If the soil is very dry, water in well and keep an eye on all newly-planted material for a few weeks, until the roots are established.

Staking and Aftercare

Staking is normally only required for trees, but certain tall shrubs and shrubs for the wall require some form of support from a strong bamboo cane or light stake. If you are planting against the wall you can use a section of trellis in wood or plastic to support your shrub. The alternative is to use wall nails and stretch a framework of wire between them. For any shrub growing on a wall or fence good support is essential, as they can grow quickly.

Generally the more care and attention you can give to your shrubs the more they will respond. Of course there are exceptions to this where perhaps you have chosen a site far too exposed for a tender shrub or perhaps the soil is too cold and heavy – in such cases all the care in the world may still lead to failure.

If you have the correct site, and have planted with care, to get the best from your new shrub some aftercare is necessary. If you are planting late in the spring or during the summer months the obvious problem to watch is watering. With the majority of shrubs growing in pots, often in a compost consisting mainly of peat, they are liable to dry out very quickly. Dry peat compost requires quite a long soak to make it thoroughly moist. Make sure that you give enough water; it is so easy to give an appearance on the surface of a well-watered shrub but if you dig down a little you may find that it is bone dry. So give plenty of water – a bucket in preference to a small can.

Many of the really successful gardens owe much to a determined programme of mulching, carried out each year. This can make the difference between success and failure. The operation of mulching involves the application of organic fibrous material as a continuous layer or mat, covering the cultivated soil. The plants feed on the slowly rotting vegetation; they get a degree of frost protection in the winter; and, perhaps most important of all, this layer helps to retain moisture during the hot summer months, allowing the shrub to have a cool moist root run. It also keeps weeds at bay.

Of course there are some shrubs which are grown in northern Europe that are quite at home in the hot dry Mediterranean regions, such as the lovely summer-flowering *Cistus* family. These are happy in the hot dry soil, but so many shrubs such as rhododendrons, azaleas and camellias suffer badly in hot dry weather and benefit enormously from plenty of mulch.

The optimum time to apply your mulch is in the autumn or early spring while the soil is damp. It is possible to use a selection of materials, either home-produced or bought from your garden centre or shop. In recent years coarse ground bark has become very popular, as this makes an excellent mulch. Another excellent material is dry bracken, when stacked and allowed to break down. You can also use pine needles, if plentiful, or leaf mould. Leaves collected in the autumn can also be used but perhaps are best heaped for a few months as they blow about too much when dry. Any form of good garden compost can be used as a mulch, including some well-rotted manure. Moss peat can be used but it dries out in the summer and can be difficult to get wet again. Grass mowings are not very suitable as they form a rather wet soggy mass. Another material formerly used was spent hops, the waste from breweries. This material was excellent but is now in short supply. Whatever you choose make a layer 1 – 1 ½ in (5 – 6 cm) deep around the base of your plant. On well-established shrubs you can increase this to 6 in (15 cm).

So apart from ensuring that your new shrubs are well watered and free from pests, aftercare should not be too onerous. Avoid any deep cultivation around the base of your shrubs as many will have a mass of roots near the surface. Above all do not forget the mulch.

Fertilisers and Manures

Well-established healthy shrubs require little in the way of fertiliser, in fact too much nitrogen can encourage an excess of growth at the expense of flowers.

I have already stressed the value of mulching. In the early spring I usually give a light dressing of sulphate of ammonia to all the lime-hating subjects such as rhododendrons, azaleas and camellias. This is a quick-acting high nitrogen fertiliser that will also increase soil acidity. I would recommend a very light dressing of about 1 oz per sq. yd. (35 g per m²). For plants that do not require an acid soil a light dressing of balanced granular fertiliser will also help to keep shrubs in good condition but again keep the rate to about 1 oz (35 g).

Always apply any fertiliser in the early spring when the plant can gain full benefit from the various nutrients. In autumn, especially at planting time, the very slow-acting bone meal can be useful (one exception being the lime-hating shrubs, as bone meal can increase the lime content in your soil).

To sum up, use plenty of humus when you plant in the form of peat, well-rotted compost or bark, mulch well and fertilise sparingly. So often a sad struggling shrub is not suffering from lack of feed but either poor drainage or being in a part of the garden near to large trees where the ground becomes as dry as a desert in the summer. No amount of fertiliser or mulch will solve these problems – the only answer here is to find a new site.

Pruning

In many commercial shrub growing nurseries it is necessary to develop stock beds or hedges of various shrubs to supply the necessary cuttings for propagation. One essential operation for the commercial grower is to make sure that the shrubs are well pruned each year, ensuring plenty of healthy new growth. These commercial stock beds produce some of the most compact free-flowering shrubs which indicates that in many cases amateur gardeners neglect the operation of pruning.

If there is one activity that is guaranteed to give rise to some confusion it is pruning. This is totally understandable as we are dealing with a varied selection of plants that all have different requirements. In pruning, the aim is to encourage healthy vigorous growth, to keep a good shape and to encourage the maximum amount of flowers or in some cases young foliage. To achieve this result we have again to follow certain rules.

1   The aim of all reputable nurserymen is to sell you a bushy well-branched young plant that should require little initial pruning. If in fact you have bought a thin leggy specimen, early pruning is vital to get the basic structure correct.

2   Evergreen shrubs are generally fairly slow-growing and in many cases require no pruning. If perhaps a rhododendron or camellia has got out of shape or too large, it is best to carry out any pruning early in the spring. A few of the more vigorous evergreens, such as *Escallonia* or *Berberis*, should be pruned fairly hard after they have finished flowering.

3   Deciduous shrubs that flower on growth made in the current growing season, which include many summer-flowering shrubs such as *Hypericum* 'Hidcote', *Buddleia* and *Spiraea* 'Anthony Waterer', should all be pruned hard in winter to early spring giving maximum time for new growth to develop.

4   Deciduous shrubs which flower on new shoots produced during the previous year are in many cases spring-flowering and should be cut back immediately after flowering. Typical examples here are the yellow *Forsythia* and the sweet-smelling Mock Orange *Philadelphus*.

The tools required to carry out any pruning are a sharp pair of secateurs and a light pruning saw for heavy branches. Many gardeners advocate using a sharp knife, but pruning is one operation during which it is very easy to slip and cut yourself. An antifungal substance will be required to aid major plant wounds to avoid infection. It is most important to ensure that any cuts you make are clean leaving no ragged edges and torn pieces – otherwise possible die-back and disease may occur.

In any pruning operation the first thing to do is to remove any dead or diseased twigs and branches. Then, depending on what you are aiming to achieve, prune to help the structure of your shrub or encourage new growth.

One of the commonest questions is 'Where should I actually cut the plant?' If there is an obvious outward-facing bud prune just above this: the reason being that it is better to keep an open structure on any plant with branches growing outwards rather than through the bush. On some shrubs it is in fact very hard to identify a bud: in such cases the answer is to prune the shrub as you think necessary, ignoring inward or outward-facing buds.

With deciduous shrubs be bold. Cut a *Philadelphus* or *Forsythia* back really hard and you will be amazed at the transformation next spring. There are so many shrubs that really are not giving of their best, and in such cases a really hard cut-back at the correct moment would both transform the vigour and certainly give more colour.

One essential aspect of pruning is to learn more about the various shrubs that we grow. When do they flower? On current or last year's growth? Are your evergreens fast or slow-growing? With this basic knowledge (see Part III) much of the fear and mystery can soon be removed.

Pests and Diseases

If there is one big advantage to be gained from growing shrubs it is that they are usually trouble-free, giving many years of pleasure with a minimum of problems.

Nevertheless, shrubs do suffer from some ailments. In most cases this is due to early frost damage on young shoots, poor drainage, very dry conditions or acid-loving plants growing in alkaline soil. It is quite rare to find a shrub that has actually died as a result of a pest or disease, but it would be wrong to suggest that they do not exist; therefore it may be helpful to know how to tackle the problem.

I certainly do not advocate the indiscriminate use of chemicals around the garden; with modern methods of application by aerosol or small sprayer it is all too easy to apply these chemicals with little thought of any damage to the beneficial insects. If, for argument's sake, we spray to kill greenfly and at the same time kill all the ladybirds, the one insect that really helps us has been destroyed.

It would be nice to return to the old days when few chemicals were used and pests were controlled by natural methods, but at least over the past few years there has been a vast improvement on the type of spray used, with many insecticides now based on the extract of *Pyrethrum* flowers.

If you go into your local garden centre or shop there is often a confusing selection of bottles and powders available for almost every ailment. The problem is that every major manufacturer of garden chemicals produces perhaps a spray to kill greenfly and naturally they want to sell their own product which they give a brand name, it could be Tumblebug, Sprayday or perhaps Kil. In many cases you will find that all these sprays contain exactly the same chemical; therefore my advice is to look carefully at the details on the bottle or pack as this may help you through the confusion of brand names.

Pests

Aphids (Greenfly)

These are certainly the most common of all our insect pests; in some years they can become a plague and do considerable damage. Above all, encourage the ladybirds in your garden, as they feed on greenfly. In fact it is possible now for commercial growers to buy specially-bred ladybirds, wasps and others which can be introduced into a glasshouse full of plants to devour all harmful insects. No doubt in years to come there will also be more emphasis on biological control in the garden.

Greenfly suck the juices from a plant feeding on the fresh young spring growth. If they are not controlled the result is pale distorted shoots and damaged flower buds. My advice if you have a bad attack is to spray with one of the *Pyrethrum*-based sprays; if necessary repeat again in 7 – 10 days until all greenfly have disappeared.

Birds

Birds are not really a pest, but they can be a nuisance, when, for example, a flock of bullfinches appear to strip the flower buds from a favourite shrub or fruit tree. They are also partial to many of the autumn berries on shrubs such as pyracantha and cotoneaster. There are various bird repellent sprays on the market, which are quite harmless to the birds and just make the berries taste rather nasty. Apart from this you can net some of the more vulnerable shrubs during the winter or early spring months, but this can be rather cumbersome.

Caterpillars

These can sometimes be a problem, especially the smaller ones from certain members of the moth family. With the present decline in the butterfly population, however, one is keen to encourage them to breed and increase their numbers. If you leave a wild patch in the garden with a few stinging nettles for the butterflies to breed, then the caterpillars should not trouble your shrubs. If they really do become a problem then use a spray containing the chemical Gamma HCH and Derris.

Red Spider Mite

Red Spider is not a common problem in garden shrubs, but it can occur. A mass of these small mites attack the underside of leaves; the first symptoms are pale or mottled leaves. If you suspect this problem pick a leaf and look at it under a magnifying glass. You may then see the mass of small red insects that are causing the problem. Spray with a strong systemic insecticide containing the chemical dimethoate.

Scale Insects

Scale insects are fortunately not too common, but they are quite difficult to eradicate. This pest is most common on camellias, and the first tell-tale sign of trouble is a black sooty mould that appears on the upper side of the leaves. This mould forms on the sticky substance produced by the scale. Underneath the leaf you will find a small brown limpet-like creature, which can best be described as a greenfly with a shell on. As with the more common greenfly, scale will suck the goodness from the leaves leaving the shrub looking pale and sick.

If you find this problem, spray with insecticide based on Malathion, taking care to spray thoroughly underneath the leaves. At least two sprays at around 10 days' interval are required to kill scale. To remove the black sooty mould try one of the proprietary leaf cleaners or soft soap and warm water.

Slugs and Snails

If aphids are the number one pest then slugs and snails must be number two. Fortunately they have a preference for herbaceous plants and young

vegetables but certainly young shrubs can be quite vulnerable. Slugs do most damage at night, disappearing to a quiet cool spot during the day.

Slug pellets are definitely effective, yet there is a fear that other creatures might also eat them. Slug-killing sprays work well.

Vine Weevils

The adult vine weevil is a small black beetle. It lays eggs in the soil which hatch out to become small dirty white grubs which attack certain shrubs at ground level and eat all round the bark causing the plant to collapse and die suddenly. If this happens, dig up the plant and see if there is any damage at the base. The grubs usually attack in the early spring and in most cases the damage is done before you are aware of it.

In summer the adult beetles hatch out and then proceed to attack the leaves, leaving tell-tale half-moon cuts in the leaf. They particularly like rhododendron leaves. This is not an easy one to control; all you can do is dust the leaves with Gamma Dust in the summer in order to deter the adult beetle.

Tortrix Moth

This can be rather deceptive as there is apparently no sign of any insect. Eggs of the tortrix moth hatch out and develop into a small green or brown caterpillar. Each caterpillar spins a fine web of hairs around the young leaves of a suitable host plant making the leaf or group of leaves into a small parcel. If you open this with care inside you will find the small caterpillar which feeds on the leaves. Japanese evergreen azaleas can be attacked mainly during early summer. If it is only a mild attack, remove the caterpillar, plus the leaves. For a bad attack, use a spray with an insecticide containing Gamma HCH and derris.

Diseases and Disorders

Bark Split

After a very cold winter certain shrubs can be damaged with bark split, and in some cases this is so severe that the whole plant often collapses and dies without the true reasons being discovered. If you notice any signs of bark split after the winter, cut out the badly-affected branches back to healthy bark. Rhododendrons and azaleas are particularly vulnerable.

Coral Spot

This fungus is seen only on dead wood. Rather attractive coral pink spots appear on the dead stems or branches. As the spores are airborne, it is wise to treat any large pruning cuts with a suitable dressing to avoid infection. At the first signs of coral spot cut out all diseased and dead branches.

Galls

These are normally only seen on evergreen azaleas and certain dwarf rhododendrons. Ugly wart-like growths, red or green in colour, usually first noticeable in spring, appear singly on leaves, which should be picked off and burnt. The disease spreads by means of fungal spores carried by the wind and insects but it seldom amounts to a serious problem. If the plants become badly affected, spray with the chemical Zineb.

Powdery Mildew

There are certain shrubs that can suffer badly from mildew in various forms; many of the roses we grow are certainly common victims. The usual symptoms are patches of powdery white dust starting on the young shoots and eventually spreading to much of the plant. Avoid planting your shrubs too close as this can encourage the problem. To control mildew, spray with a systemic fungicide containing benomyl. Some shrubs such as the small-leaved *Euonymus fortunei* 'Emerald and Gold' can be affected so badly that the plant has to be destroyed. If any badly-diseased shoots are apparent in the autumn cut them off.

Weed Control

In the section on planting the importance of ensuring that the ground is really clean before you start a new shrub border was stressed, as it is so much easier to remove perennial weeds such as ground elder, couch or sorrel from clear ground. Once you have established shrubs these persistent weeds are really difficult to eradicate.

The most obvious way to control weeds is to cultivate the soil with a hoe or similar cultivator, but be careful around many of the surface-rooting shrubs. In addition you may have bulbs or herbaceous plants growing among the shrubs, making cultivation difficult.

Applying a good mulch over a border can also keep weeds at bay; coarse ground bark is particularly suitable, as it shows the shrubs off well, keeps in moisture and will suppress the growth of many weeds. Also, where you have a persistent weed such as ground elder, applying a mulch on top of it will encourage this naturally surface-rooting weed to root up in the mulch, making it very much easier to remove. One interesting remedy for a small shrub border infested with ground elder involved removing all the shrubs, and covering the whole bed in black polythene, which was buried at the edges. Holes were then cut in the polythene and various shrubs replanted. Finally the whole area was covered in a layer of peat giving the appearance of a very clean border.

If all else fails there are a number of very useful weedkillers on the market that can help to keep your borders clean. Here are a few that may prove useful. They are listed under their chemical name.

Alloxydim Sodium

This is often sold under the brand name of 'Weedout'. It is an interesting new material designed to kill most grasses, especially couch, in established shrubs. The procedure is to spray over the top of existing plants, and even where couch grass is growing among the roots of an established shrub the couch will die, but the shrub remains unharmed. One word of warning with this weedkiller is to avoid spraying on or near any of your ornamental grasses.

Glysophate

In the UK this is generally sold under the brand name of 'Tumbleweed'. When sprayed on to growing weeds it is absorbed by the plant tissue which will gradually change colour and eventually die; this whole process may take up to two weeks. The great advantage of Glysophate-based weedkillers is that they will kill persistent weeds such as couch grass, creeping buttercup and with perhaps two or more applications ground elder. It can be very useful to clean up a border prior to planting as there is no lasting residual effect in the soil. What of course is most important is to avoid spraying any green parts of your shrubs, otherwise they will suffer.

Paraquat

This is often sold under the trade name of 'Weedol'. It is a very dangerous product in concentrated form and in common with all weedkillers should be stored carefully away from the reach of children. Paraquat acts quickly to kill many annual weeds. Again there is no lasting residual effect on the soil. Unfortunately it will burn but not kill many of the more persistent weeds. Again avoid splashing any on the foliage of surrounding shrubs.

Simazine

Simazine is often sold under the brand name of 'Weedex'. In commercial horticulture this is one of the most useful chemicals for keeping fields of trees and shrubs weedfree for up to 12 months. It is a chemical that will not kill any existing weed and must therefore be applied to completely clean ground early in the spring. It remains active in the top layers of the soil for up to 12 months, preventing any further weed germination. Unfortunately there are a number of shrubs that can be affected by this product, therefore it should be confined to non-growing areas such as paths and drives.

These few weedkillers will certainly play a useful role in the garden, if used sensibly, bearing in mind that the shrubs are as vulnerable as the weeds you aim to kill. There are also some useful selective weedkillers based generally on the chemical 2-4D often sold under the brand names of 'Verdone' and 'Supertox'. This is the weedkiller that is mainly used to kill daisies and plantains in your lawn. It can also be useful for killing patches of bad perennial weed, such as nettles; but use it with extreme care, and choose a still day, as this is a volatile material that drifts and can harm nearby shrubs.

Part II
PROPAGATION

Introduction

With modern equipment and the chemicals now available, the opportunities to propagate shrubs from seed, cuttings or (if you are really keen) grafting, have improved enormously. Hormone rooting powders, well-balanced composts, plastic trays and small propagators act as useful aids but, despite this help, success is never guaranteed, which makes for a stimulating challenge, One year a certain batch of cuttings will root with almost 100 per cent success, but try again the following year at the same time with the same techniques and you may well get 100 per cent failure.

Of course the type of equipment required will depend very much on how many cuttings you are likely to take. Equipment can consist of as little as one old yogurt pot on the windowsill for stage one. There are available from garden centres and shops a wide range of plastic propagators which consist of a simple seed tray with a clear plastic lid to fit over the top. The ultimate in small propagators has built-in electric heating cables controlled by a thermostat. These certainly speed up the rooting and allow you to propagate more difficult shrubs – but up go your costs! If you really get bitten by the propagation bug you can set up a small heated bench in a glasshouse complete with automatic misting equipment. This will give you a scaled-down version of the large commercial propagating houses used at the majority of shrub nurseries.

A commercial nursery producing shrubs and trees will probably employ the following methods to produce young plants; cuttings; seed; grafting; budding and layering.

For the majority of enthusiasts, cuttings and seed will probably cover most everyday needs. Layering, a technique not used so much now, can be very useful to produce perhaps the odd special rhododendron or azalea; it is slow but requires little attention after the initial preparation. Budding and grafting are really for the specialist, but for enthusiasts they can still be carried out on a small scale.

Cuttings

For anyone keen to root just a few of their favourite shrubs this is without doubt the most useful method of propagation. Many plants root with comparative ease if some fairly simple rules are followed.

1   The majority of cuttings are just a short length of plant material without any roots, therefore in the early stages it is essential to have a warm moist atmosphere to encourage rooting. If a cutting becomes dry or exposed to unnecessary draughts it will almost certainly fail. Small modern propagators with their plastic lids are designed specifically to create this moist, draught-free atmosphere.

2   Rooting medium. One aspect of propagation that gives rise to many failures is poor rooting medium. The basic requirement is for a well-drained open medium with plenty of air in the soil. A medium which will suit most plants is a 50/50 mix of sphagnum moss peat and perlite. A good sharp sand can be a substitute for perlite but if you use sand make sure it is really gritty, and if you are rooting any lime-haters such as heathers or azaleas make sure the sand is free of lime. I would strongly advise you against using garden soil. After many weeks of constant watering this will pack down hard, excluding all the air which is certain failure for most cuttings. Avoid the soft types of sand often used by builders as this will also pack down very hard.

    The dark black sedge peat is far too fine in texture for propagation, and sphagnum peat will give you far better results.

3   Hormone rooting powder. This is a useful aid to encourage roots. The hormone ingredient in these powders stimulates the cutting both to root faster and to produce more roots. It would be wrong to say that powders are always necessary, as many plants will root well without them, but they can help and for difficult subjects they are essential. Powders are sold in three different strengths. Seradix is probably the most widely used powder, with Seradix 1 the weakest for use with very soft cuttings. Medium strength Seradix 2 is for semi-ripe cuttings and the strongest, Seradix 3 is for hardwood cuttings.

    These powders are more than 90 per cent talcum powder, so ensure that plenty sticks to the cuttings. The best way is to dampen the cuttings prior to inserting them in the hormone powder. When you insert the cuttings into your rooting medium do not just push them in, as this will remove much of the powder. Use a small cane or plastic dibber to make a hole first, then insert the cutting and very lightly firm or water in.

When you have the correct conditions, an open well-drained rooting medium, and some hormone rooting powder, you can turn to the cuttings themselves.

A cutting is defined in the Royal Horticultural Society's *Dictionary of Gardening* as: 'any portion or a plant root, stem, leaf or bud which is separated from the plant and has been induced to produce roots of its own'. Cuttings are commonly described according to their state of growth.

1   Softwood cuttings. These are the first flush of growth that arrives in the spring and early summer. Generally these young fresh cuttings root quickly but in such a soft state require exceptionally moist, warm conditions to prevent wilting.

2   Semi-ripe cuttings. This is perhaps the most productive time, once the new growth begins

to ripen around mid-summer. Temperatures are high, the light is good, and a dip into No. 2 strength of rooting hormone should ensure a fairly high degree of success.

3   Ripe or hardwood cuttings. During late autumn and winter hard ripe material is produced. To achieve success with evergreens will often require extra heat to encourage rooting. Many of the common hedging and screening evergreens such as laurel and privet will root from winter hardwood cuttings without extra heat, and this can also apply to many ornamental conifers which root late autumn to early winter without heat. The more unusual shrubs such as rhododendrons and camellias root from hardwood cuttings, but will normally fail to root without extra heat from electric cables or similar. Many deciduous shrubs such as *Deutzia, Forsythia, Philadelphus* and *Weigela* will root from 6 – 8 inch (15.5 – 20 cm) lengths of hardwood stem lined out across the garden over winter. Left in situ until the following spring you can achieve good results.

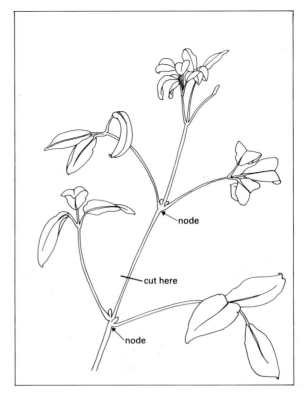

Fig. 1 An internodal cutting.

The next important consideration is selection of the right piece of plant material to remove from the bush. Here again we have various types of cutting depending on how and where we finally cut them. Where the leaves join the stem is known as the node. If cut at this point the cutting is called a nodal cutting. If cut between two sets of leaves this is described as internodal (see Fig. 1). The third type is a leaf bud cutting, which can be used successfully on camellias, mahonias and magnolias. Here we have a small section of stem 1 – 2 in long (2.5 – 5 cm), including a set of leaves with a potential bud in the leaf axil.

Much has been written and discussed in the past about taking a cutting with a 'heel'. My personal opinion is that this is not really very important: a good healthy young shoot cut either at a node or between two nodes will usually root given correct treatment. Of course, there are exceptions, especially with shrubs which are always difficult to propagate.

A few essential points to consider before you remove any cuttings are as follows.

1   Make sure the plant is healthy and vigorous. You will achieve poor results from old tired shrubs.

2   Make sure the plant is true to name and propagate from the best form available, i.e. good colour and large flowers.

3   Always take cuttings from healthy shoots of current season's growth.

When you remove the cutting from your tree or shrub use a sharp knife or secateurs. Never insert cuttings with damaged leaves as these encourage disease. Reduce the number of leaves on your cutting to four or five but do not cut leaves in half as this again creates a wound that lets in disease. In a few cases a light wound with a sharp knife or potato peeler prior to inserting in the hormone powder will aid rooting.

If the cuttings are soft it is wise to cut them early in the morning or late at night when the atmosphere is cool. Avoid the heat of the day as they will wilt very quickly.

Around 3 – 4 in long (7.5 – 10 cm) is ideal for most cuttings. Prepare them quickly with a sharp knife and insert them into a suitable pot or box filled with the correct rooting medium. Water in well to settle the compost around the cutting – but do not firm. Place in warm close conditions. Please resist the temptation to pull the cutting out every few days hoping to see roots!

Aftercare of Cuttings

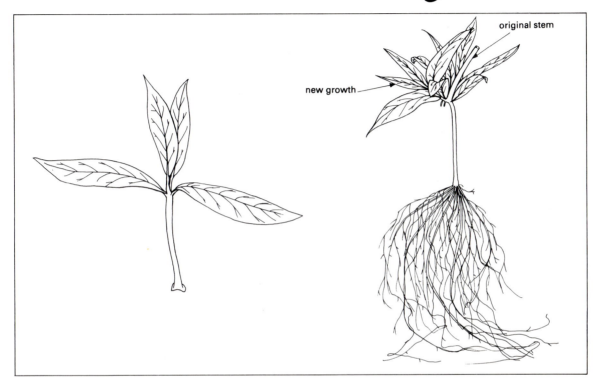

new growth

original stem

Fig. 2 A semi-ripe nodal cutting of *Weigela* taken in summer (left) and rooted ready for potting-on in the following spring (right).

The warm moist atmosphere we aim to create for our cuttings unfortunately also provides ideal conditions for certain common plant diseases to thrive. The fungal diseases such as botrytis can quickly sweep through a batch of cuttings resulting in total loss. To avoid this problem follow these simple rules.

1   Never use diseased or damaged material.

2   Keep your propagating equipment sterilised and clean.

3   Inspect the cuttings every 7 – 10 days and remove any dead cuttings and fallen leaves.

4   Every 10 – 14 days drench with a suitable fungicide such as Benlate or Captan.

When it is fairly obvious that your cuttings are well rooted (see Fig. 2), remove them to a more bracing atmosphere to allow them to 'harden off' – a term used to indicate the transition from warm soft growing conditions to the weather these plants are likely to find in the garden. Obviously if weather conditions outside are cold and frosty, it will be necessary to give your cuttings some protection in a cool greenhouse or cold frame with the aim of putting them out when spring arrives.

From the pot or tray where the cuttings are rooted the cuttings should be potted on into a 3 in (7.5 cm) pot, enabling you to establish a small plant that will survive outside in your garden if planted during good growing conditions.

This potting-on is in fact a crucial stage in propagation and there are many failures at this point. Again, here are a few rules.

1   Use a compost that is fairly low in fertiliser.

2   Do not overpot; a 3 in (7.5 cm) pot will be large enough for nearly all shrubs.

3   Try to carry out your potting if possible in early spring through to the end of summer. Avoid autumn and winter as with failing light and dropping temperatures you will get little growth. It is better to leave your cuttings in the box or pot through the winter with a view to potting on in early spring.

Once the plants are established, begin to apply a weak liquid feed during the growing season, and a little pinching of shoots that grow away can start a framework of a good bushy shrub.

Seeds

This method of propagation can be useful for a limited range of shrubs, but apart from the fact that many actually fail to set any seed at all it is slow and may take many years to produce a flowering plant.

On the other hand there are certain plants that are exceptionally difficult to root from cuttings but are quite easy to grow from seed. One example is the lovely purple or sometimes white early spring flowering *Daphne mezereum*. If you can keep the birds off the seeds, which turn bright red like redcurrants in the summer, collect and sow the seed immediately in a well-drained gritty mix with no fertiliser; you should then get a fairly good rate of germination the following spring.

One word of warning – do remember that many of the shrubs in our gardens are hybrids, i.e. the results of cross-breeding between two species. For example, many of the lovely rhododendrons that we know and enjoy have resulted from a cross of a certain species perhaps found wild high in the Himalayas with an existing garden plant. The seedlings produced from such a cross are grown on until they flower, and then perhaps one is selected as a new and exciting hybrid. If you collect and sow seed from a hybrid shrub you have no guarantee that the resulting plant will grow true – in fact you have every chance of a complete mixture of colours. So it is only really safe to grow from seed from a known true species.

If you do plan to try to propagate a few shrubs from seed, always collect your own fresh seed. So often seed purchased from other sources has been allowed to dry out and will give poor results. The majority of shrub seeds are best sown immediately they are gathered, but if it is necessary to store them find a cool dry place and keep them in a clean container.

Many shrub seeds undergo a period of dormancy during the winter; this ensures that germination only occurs under favourable

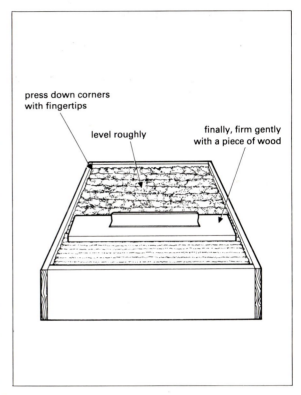

press down corners with fingertips

level roughly

finally, firm gently with a piece of wood

Fig. 3 Preparing the seed box or tray.

conditions. In order to encourage germination certain seeds should be sown in pots or trays which are plunged into the ground outside and subjected to the winter weather. As spring arrives, start to look for signs of germination and bring the pots or trays into a cool glasshouse, or put them in a cold frame. Again, a few simple rules will help you to succeed with your seed sowing.

1   Use a simple well-drained compost; 50/50 sharp sand and sphagnum peat will do well. Do not add fertiliser at this stage.

2   Use a pot or tray with plenty of drainage (see Fig. 3), as few plants will germinate well under waterlogged conditions.

3   Sow your seed as soon as it is ripe. Where possible, remove the fruity covering from such seed as that of *Berberis darwinii* – rubbing with some very sharp sand can help.

4   Above all, be patient. Shrub seeds can be very slow, sometimes taking up to two years to germinate.

Once you have a well established pot or tray of seedlings these should be potted into small pots of around 3 in (7.5 cm). Handle the delicate roots with great care, potting into compost which is fairly low in fertiliser – John Innes or one of the many proprietary peat-based composts. Make sure that the newly-potted seedlings do not dry out, and shade them from bright sun if you are using a greenhouse or frame.

As with cuttings it is wise to pot your seedlings in spring through to summer. If not potted by the end of the summer, they are best left until the following year.

Certain shrubs produced from seed, such as the *Berberis* famly, can grow away with considerable speed, but others such as rhododendrons and deciduous azaleas will germinate quite readily but may take four or five years to produce a flowering plant.

The following shrubs can be successfully grown from seed.

Acer palmatum
Acer palmatum
  varieties
Arbutus unedo
Azaleas, deciduous
Berberis darwinii
Berberis thunbergii
  atropurpurea
Daphne in variety
Ilex aquifolium
Kalmia latifolia
Lavandula
Mahonia aquifolium
Pittosporum
  tenuifolium
Rhododendrons
Spartium junceum

Here are some helpful guidelines for growing your shrubs from seed.

1   Beat the birds! They are partial to many seeds.

2   Try to make sure that any seed is fresh – which ideally means collecting your own.

3   Remove the flesh from berry-like seeds such as those of *Pittosporum*. If left on, it can inhibit germination. Do this by keeping the fleshy seeds together in a polythene bag for a few days, and when they begin to ripen add in some coarse sand. By working the mixture through your hands, the flesh can be rubbed off.

4   Sow fine seeds like those of azaleas and *Kalmia* onto the surface of the compost and simply press down. Do not cover them. These two are best sown in early spring.

5   The majority of other seeds should be sown as soon as collected into pots or boxes. Leave them outdoors over the winter but bring them into gentle heat in the spring when germination can be fairly rapid.

Grafting

Grafting is a method of uniting two pieces of closely-related plant material. Compatible plant tissue correctly joined will callous and grow together. The object of grafting is to produce a shrub that will not come true from seed and is very difficult to raise from cuttings, and sometimes we can use grafting to produce a more vigorous plant. For example, the lovely winter witch hazel *Hamamelis mollis*, and the pale yellow form 'Pallida', will not root and grow easily from cuttings, and their seed will not germinate true to colour, so the only satisfactory method of propagation is grafting.

The process involves a rootstock and a 'scion', or small length of twig, from the shrub you wish to propagate (see Fig. 4). In the case of the winter witch hazel *Hamamalis mollis*, the wild *Hamamelis virginiana* is used, because of its vigorous growing properties. From the bark and leaves of this same plant we obtain the medicinal solution Witch Hazel. This shrub, found wild in America, is grown from seed, potted and grown on into a small plant of about 12 – 18 in high (30 – 45 cm) with a stem of thickness somewhere between a knitting needle and a pencil. Then choose a 4 – 5 in (10 – 12.5 cm) length of twig or 'scion' from *Hamamelis mollis*. The diameter of the stem should be as nearly as possible identical to that of the rootstock. Then with a very sharp knife the rootstock and scion are trimmed to a shape allowing both cut surfaces to meet as

Fig. 4 A simple method of grafting.

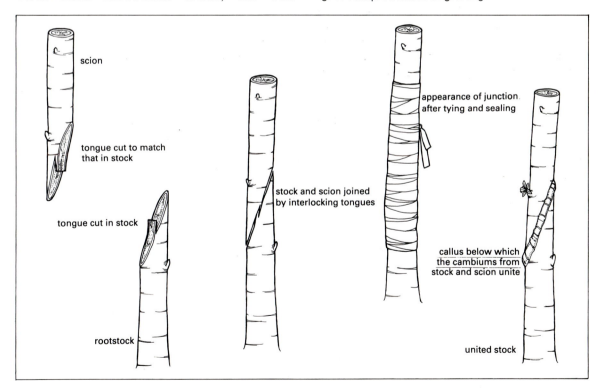

scion

tongue cut to match
that in stock

tongue cut in stock

rootstock

stock and scion joined
by interlocking tongues

appearance of junction
after tying and sealing

callus below which
the cambiums from
stock and scion unite

united stock

closely as possible. When this is done they are bound together with grafting tape, which usually consists of thin strips of flat elastic. The whole plant is then placed in a warm damp atmosphere and kept well watered.

With luck, in a few weeks scar tissue will form. A number of weeks later the two pieces will have joined firmly together, leaving you with the vigorous roots of *H. virginiana* and, after some trimming, the free-flowering top of the lovely winter-flowering *H. mollis*.

One big problem with all grafted plants is the production of suckers. Hybrid roses are perhaps the best example of this; shoots continue to grow from the original rootstock and if not removed (ideally by pulling them off) eventually they can overrun the whole plant, leaving a rather boring rootstock and a dead hybrid that you had hoped to grow and enjoy. So watch out for these suckers and remove them immediately.

Budding

This is a method of propagation used widely by commercial growers to produce many ornamental trees, fruit trees and roses. It is in fact a form of grafting, but instead of using a 3 – 4 in (7.5 – 10 cm) scion to graft on to the rootstock just one small bud is used.

Nearly all the spring-flowering cherries are produced by budding. Instead of growing the rootstock in a pot as described for the winter-flowering witch hazel, for the cherries rootstocks of the common single white-flowered *Prunus* 'Avium' or more commonly named 'Gean' are planted. Seedlings about 12 – 18 in high (30 – 45 cm) are lined out across some clean ground during the autumn, the object being to produce a small healthy young plant with a stem about as thick as a pencil. In the following summer, these rootstocks are ready for grafting.

The technique is relatively simple, requiring a very sharp knife, keen eye and a strong back if you are likely to bud shrubs in any quantity! For example, to 'bud' a few trees of the double pink cherry 'Pink Perfection' cut off from the mother tree a 'bud stick' – a length of the current year's growth, fairly ripe with a number of leaves and buds. Remove all the leaves and at each junction where the leaf joined the stem there is a bud. With a very sharp knife you cut about ½ in (1.25 cm) of bark, going behind the bud (see Fig. 5). Prior to this you have removed a similar piece of bark from the rootstock about 3 in (7.5 cm) from the ground. With great care you then place the small length of bark plus bud (called a 'bud shield') from *Prunus* 'Pink Perfection' into the cut area of your rootstock. Make sure that all edges line up as accurately as possible, then bind tightly together with grafting tape (see Fig. 6).

If successful, within about six weeks the small sliver of bark with its bud will form scar tissue and callous onto the rootstock. The grafting tape is removed when a firm union is established, and

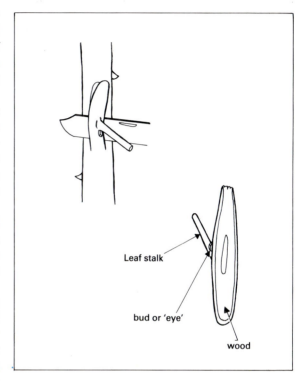

Fig. 5 Cutting the 'bud shield' from the bud stick.

everything is left until the following spring.

As soon as the first signs of growth are evident in the following year, the top of the rootstock should be cut back with a slanting cut about 1 in (2.5 cm) above the inserted bud. This single bud will then grow away with astonishing speed producing a 5 – 6 ft (1.75 – 2 m) single stem tree in one year.

As soon as the new bud grows away make sure it is tied to a 6 ft (2 m) bamboo cane, otherwise it is very vulnerable to being broken off at the union by a strong gust of wind or perhaps even an over-energetic dog.

35

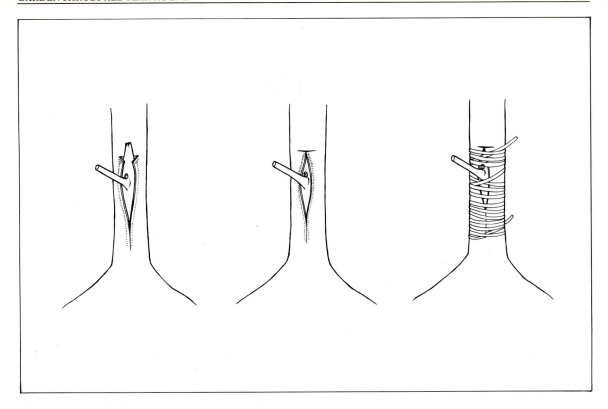

Fig. 6 Inserting the bud shield into the rootstock and binding with grafting tape.

This may all sound rather complicated, but in fact with practice this method of propagation can soon be mastered.

Layering

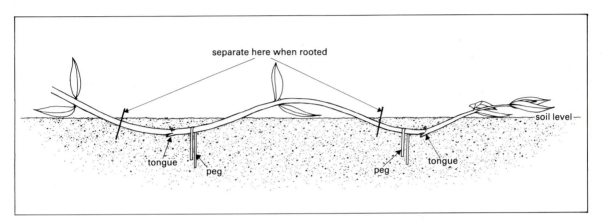

separate here when rooted

soil level —

tongue

peg

peg

tongue

Fig. 7 Pegging the layered branch to the ground.

Layering can be rather slow, but it has the advantage of being very simple and a useful way to propagate a small number of your favourite shrubs, especially the ones that are difficult to root from cuttings or to grow from seed.

If, for example, you want to produce one more plant of your favourite rhododendron, carry out the following procedure.

1   Choose a young healthy branch which is near to the ground. Something around the thickness of a pencil will be best.

2   In the area of soil where you plan to layer down your branch incorporate plenty of sphagnum peat and sharp sand mixed together.

3   Cut three small hooked wooden pegs around 9 – 12 in (23 – 30 cm) long.

4   Underneath the branch where it will touch the ground, wound very lightly with a sharp knife, and apply a quantity of strong rooting powder to this wound.

5   Using two of your wooden pegs, fix the young branch firmly to the ground (see Fig. 7), and cover for about 6 – 9 in (15 – 23 cm) of the length with the peat/sand mix about 2 in (5 cm) deep.

6   The third peg plus some strong garden twine should be used to pull the tip of your branch up to a vertical position.

As with all methods of propagation success is not guaranteed, but fairly successful results have been achieved with hybrid rhododendrons, producing a well-rooted young layer in 18 months.

When the plant has rooted well, cut the young layer from the mother plant with a pair of sharp secateurs. If the roots are definitely well established, cut around with a sharp spade and transplant the layer into some well-prepared ground.

One word of caution – sometimes the union between your new root and the stem is not very strong, so take great care whem moving the plant that all the root and soil does not fall off.

37

Part III
ALPHABETICAL LIST
OF SHRUBS

Abelia

For a shrub that will flower well up to the middle of autumn *A. × grandiflora* is one of the best; a graceful plant with brilliant green foliage turning bronze in the autumn. With modest pruning this shrub is easy to control and is especially useful for a border near a house wall. There is a variegated form which is not quite so hardy. Also worth trying is the form *A.* 'Edward Goucher' with much larger lilac pink flowers.

Abutilon

An *Abutilon* will grow quite happily fully exposed as a small tree. *A. vitifolium* is a deciduous shrub or small tree with distinctive soft furry leaves. It is a free-flowering shrub producing a mass of single flowers in shades of soft lavender, deep mauve

Abutilon vitifolium

Acer palmatum 'Dissectum'

and white. Both the blue and white forms are remarkably free-flowering and surprisingly fast-growing. Unfortunately the plants do not live very long and need to be replaced every 7 – 8 years, when they often die back and lose their vigour. Propagation is easy from cuttings taken in the spring/summer. One very attractive form of *Abutilon* is the deep blue *Abutilon × suntense* 'Jermyns', an excellent plant for a sheltered south wall.

A rather tender species from Brazil, *A. megapotamicum*, is worth trying against a south wall; the unusual bell-shaped flowers have red calyces, yellow petals and purple anthers, and the flowering period is late summer. There is also an interesting variegated form.

Acer (Maple)

This genus includes a very extensive and variable range of shrubs and trees which are generally easy to grow, given a moist rich soil and fairly sunny position. They are very useful deciduous plants for small or large gardens.

The most widely planted cultivar is *Acer palmatum* 'Atropurpureum', a Japanese Maple with deeply cut red leaves which turn a brilliant red in the autumn. It is not always an easy tree to establish, though, as it can be badly damaged by cold wind and late spring frost. Some protection in the form of a small hessian windbreak for the first year or two will help. Once established this is a very hardy tree. The very deep red form *A.p.* 'Bloodgood', and from the Trompenburg Aboretum in Holland the almost black form *A.p.* 'Trompenburg', are both very attractive.

Also from Japan are the lovely low-growing *A.p.* 'Dissectum' forms, with finely cut leaves, which give an excellent autumn display. All forms of *Acer palmatum* are rather slow-growing but well worth waiting for. The 'Dissectums' can have either green or red foliage. All these maples produce the familiar propeller-like seeds that whirl down in the autumn; if sown immediately they are collected (do not allow the seed to get dry), germination will generally occur in the spring, producing a good crop of young plants.

Amelanchier

A. laevis, a very hardy shrub or small tree, is commonly named Snowy Mespilus. In spring the bronze-coloured new leaves are quickly followed by a mass of white flowers, and as an added bonus the leaves turn to rich colours of red and gold in

41

the autumn. Eventually growing to at least 15 ft (5 m) high, this is a shrub that requires plenty of space. New shrubs can be raised from seed collected in the autumn. Unfortunately bull-finches can take a fancy to this shrub.

Arbutus

A. unedo is an interesting evergreen shrub that will grow on acid or chalky soil. It is a native of the Mediterranean and S.W. Ireland. It is commonly known as the 'Strawberry Tree', because of the attractive strawberry-like fruits that appear in the autumn. The white lily-of-the-valley like flowers often appear at the same time as the fruit, producing a lovely combination. The pink-flowered form *A.u.* 'Rubra' is very attractive. It will root from semi-ripe cuttings, but probably the easiest way to propagate is by means of seed extracted from the strawberry-like fruit.

Amelanchier laevis

Arundinaria (Bamboo)

Here is a very useful plant which surprisingly has never gained great popularity. The most widely planted, *A. japonica,* makes a wonderful screen up to 10 ft (2.4 m) high. It does not spread too fast, having a round tufted habit. For good ground cover growing to around 3½ ft (1 m) the attractive *A. variegata* with its striking dark green leaves boldly striped with white, is a very bright evergreen for a dull winter's day.

To grow bamboo successfully shelter from cold winds is essential: over-exposed plants quickly become disfigured with burnt brown leaves. Ideally plant in a rich, not too heavy, loam with plenty of moisture, and an annual dressing of well-rotted manure or compost will be beneficial.

Arbutus unedo

Propagation is best done by division, cutting small pieces off the matted roots with a sharp spade. The best time to do this is early autumn or late spring.

Aucuba

The handsome evergreen *Aucuba* is a rather old-fashioned plant, conjuring up visions of dark, dreary Victorian gardens. Unfortunately, it is one of those shrubs requiring both male and female plants to produce the distinctive bright red berries. *A. japonica* 'Crotonifolia', with its boldly speckled leaves, is an excellent shrub for keen flower arrangers, and this male form planted with the boldly marked *A.j.* 'Gold Dust' should encourage a fine crop of winter berries.

Azalea

Deciduous Azaleas

We accept without question the magnificent range of deciduous azaleas available today. Over 100 years ago in Belgium and Holland work started on the improvement of these magnificent shrubs, and crosses were made between the long flowering species from Eastern America and their European relative the Pontic Azalea, that sweet-scented yellow form. This initial work resulted in a range of azaleas called Ghent hybrids, but sadly many of these are no longer available. This I feel is very unfortunate as they were beautiful garden plants with a mass of small scented flowers and good autumn colour. A few, like the bright orange *A.* 'Coccinea Speciosa', the soft yellow *A.* 'Daviesii', or pale yellow *A. narcissiflorum* are still available.

The less flamboyant Ghent hybrids were

eclipsed by the large flowered forms raised by the Waterer family at Knaphill Nursery and the de Rothschild family at Exbury Gardens. Even today, work continues to improve the strain with excellent new hybrids being developed at the Saville Gardens at Windsor.

Deciduous azaleas are all part of the rhododendron family and therefore can only be grown on lime-free soil. If you are fortunate and have the right conditions they really are excellent garden shrubs. They are very hardy and able to withstand far more cold than their evergreen relations. Fully grown they rarely exceed 5 – 6 ft (1.75 – 2 m) in height and once established can be relied on to flower with great freedom with the added bonus of excellent autumn colour when the leaves fall.

By far the sweetest scent of all azaleas comes from the honeysuckle-shaped yellow flowers of *A. pontica* which is a native of eastern Europe, and this species also has perhaps the best autumn colour.

Deciduous azaleas, in common with all their relations in the rhododendron family, have compact fibrous root systems, with roots coming up to the surface of the soil. At planting time, incorporate plenty of moss peat into the soil or other suitable acid compost. Mulch well, and make sure that the soil does not dry out too much during the summer months.

They respond well to pruning, and this can be very important during the first year or two when it is important to develop a well-branched plant with many stems coming up from the base. I usually try to prune in late winter just before the new growth begins. A light dressing of sulphate of ammonia at 1 oz per sq. yd. (30 g per m²) applied in the spring will help to keep the plants in good condition.

To propagate deciduous azaleas from cuttings is in fact very difficult. Very soft cuttings taken in late spring will root with the aid of bottom heat; if you are successful, leave the cuttings in your tray over winter and pot them on early in the spring. By far the easiest way to increase your stock is by collecting seed in the autumn. Store this in a dry place over winter, sow it in late winter in sieved moss peat and you should see a mass of fine seedlings in around three weeks. As soon as they can be handled, prick them out into boxes and by pinching out the soft growth you can soon make quite a sturdy little plant. It usually takes a few years to develop a flowering plant.

A. 'Annabella'

Large golden yellow flowers flushed with orange rose. The deep bronze foliage contrasts very well with the yellow flowers.

A. 'Balzac'

A good, deep orange flower.

A. 'Berryrose'

A warm salmon pink with deep orange flash in the throat. The young foliage is a pale coppery red.

A. 'Coccinea Speciosa'

This is one of the old Ghent hybrids first listed in 1836. The mass of small flowers are a really intense tangerine red, unlike any other deciduous azaleas. The leaves are small, bright green and the whole shrub has an attractive spreading habit of growth. A further bonus is the advantage of flowering in summer when many of the azaleas are over.

A. 'Daviesii'

Raised over 100 years ago by Isaac Davies of Ormskirk in Lancashire, this azalea is very fragrant, the buds are buff yellow and pink at the top, and the wide flowers are first creamy white flushed with pink then slowly fade to pure white. It has a low, rather spreading habit and can be easily identified by the soft grey foliage. Sadly not too common but well worth growing if you can obtain a plant.

A. 'Gibraltar'

One of the most reliable and perhaps one of the easier ones to root from cuttings. The buds are an

Azalea pontica

attractive crimson orange, opening to large flame/orange flowers with slightly frilled petals.

A. 'Homebush'

This is an azalea of great charm with almost completely double flower heads of deep carmine rose. 'Homebush' certainly adds a different shape of flower.

A. 'Hotspur'

A strong growing, hot fiery red to deep orange flower.

A. pontica

This species is a native of Eastern Europe and the Caucasus. For a really exquisite scent this one must take first prize, and the same can be said for the magnificent display of autumn colour, when the leaves turn to brilliant shades of red and orange. What the deep yellow flowers lack in size is certainly amply compensated for by the other features. This is an easy azalea to raise from seed collected in the autumn; it is also perhaps more vigorous than certain hybrids.

A. 'Silver Slipper'

An excellent name for a beautiful azalea which has creamy white flowers with a pink flush and distinctive yellow markings in the throat.

A. 'Strawberry Ice'

Definitely one of the best and most popular of deciduous azaleas. The flower buds are red and open to a soft pink shading to a slightly darker

45

GARDEN SHRUBS ALL YEAR ROUND

colour on the edge of the petals. 'Strawberry Ice' has pronounced yellow markings in the throat.

Evergreen Japanese Azaleas

In the past 50 – 60 years an amazing number of hardy evergreen azaleas have been raised, giving now a bewildering range to choose from. As the name clearly implies the majority are native to Japan. Considerable breeding work was carried out primarily by nurserymen in Holland who produced some of the lovely hybrids we grow today.

The evergreen azalea is part of the rhododendron family and requires very similar growing conditions. Most importantly azaleas, as with rhododendrons, will only grow in an acid soil; any lime present will soon make the foliage turn yellow and the shrub will eventually die. To overcome this problem it is possible to grow these lovely shrubs in pots or tubs, but make sure that these are filled with acid compost.

As a compact, low-growing evergreen on average 2 – 3 ft (60 – 90 cm) high, this has proved to be an excellent shrub for the small garden and can also be used with dramatic effect where mass planting is carried out on a larger scale. Another plus for this family is the very reliable way they produce a mass of flowers each year; in many cases the flowers are borne so freely that all the leaves are smothered. The description 'evergreen' is not always true, because a number such as the lovely large flowered white A. 'Palestrina' do shed a lot of leaves in the winter, whereas other varieties such as the bright red A. 'Hinodegiri' (Red Hussar) certainly retain their foliage throughout the year. A few hybrids also have quite good autumn colour, giving an extra bonus.

If available, choose an area of the garden with light shade, and not too dry, and add plenty of humus in the form of moss peat, leafmould or spent hops. Azaleas will grow quite happily in full sun, the drawback being that many flowers can fade rapidly in a spell of sunny weather. As they flower in the spring, they are susceptible to late frost, so an area of light shade will certainly help to protect the flowers from this problem.

With fine fibrous roots which come right up to the surface, azaleas can suffer badly in dry weather. If you mulch well with peat, bark or bracken this will be a great help. Avoid using the hoe too near as the fine surface roots will certainly be damaged; mulching and weeding by hand is the best solution. It may be necessary to give your plants a light prune, particularly in the early stages, to form a good-shaped plant; carry this out after flowering and the plant will respond. This is one of the very easy shrubs to raise from cuttings. Take young shoots from current season's growth about 2 – 3 in long (5 – 7.5 cm) trim off a few of the bottom leaves, and add hormone rooting powder of a medium strength (but it is not essential). Put in a rooting medium of 50/50 moss peat and sharp sand and in 8 – 10 weeks you should have plenty of well-rooted cuttings ready to pot on in the spring.

There are so many hybrids now available ranging in various flower shapes and colours covering white, pink, red, scarlet and lavender. Try to select the colours with some care as indiscriminate planting of all the colours can be rather overwhelming.

A. 'Apple Blossom'

A mass of small flowers on a compact bush with round pale green leaves; as the name implies, the flowers combine the colours of pink and white very much like spring apple blossom.

A. 'Blaauw's Pink'

This form has a fairly upright habit of growth and is quite vigorous, with a mass of dark green leaves. The flowers are very deep pink and double.

A. 'Blue Danube'

The name is somewhat misleading as the colour of the large flowers is in fact a deep bluish violet, which is a change from many of the azalea colours. 'Blue Danube' makes a fairly open bush, and planted near to a white azalea this hybrid gives a lovely combination of colour.

Azalea 'Blue Danube'

46

A. 'Hinodegiri' (Red Hussar)

Probably one of the most widely planted of all evergreen azaleas, it is free-flowering, with a low compact habit. The mass of bright crimson flowers can totally smother the foliage, and many of the leaves turn bright red giving an added bonus in the autumn.

A. 'Hinomayo'

With beautiful clear pink single flowers, this hybrid always looks delicate but in fact can stand a lot of cold winter weather. Definitely one of the best to include in any collection of azaleas. It will often shed most of its summer leaves, producing a fresh flush the following spring.

A. 'Iro-hayama'

This has a refreshing colour among so many bright red and crimson azaleas. A low dense shrub with pale green leaves, in spring the whole plant is a mass of small white flowers tinged with lavender.

A. 'Kirin'

Pretty little double pink flowers. This is one of the hybrids that is often sold in early spring as an indoor flowering plant. Potted up in the autumn and forced early with a little gentle heat it will flower happily in late winter/early spring.

A. 'Leo'

This attractive azalea, with large soft orange flowers, has the great advantage of extending the flowering season to the end of spring and even into early summer. The flowering season for most azaleas is over by the middle of spring so this spreading hybrid 'Leo' makes a welcome addition.

A. 'Mother's Day'

This is one of the very best dwarf evergreen azaleas. The flowers are very large, dark red and semi-double and contrast well with the foliage, which is a dark, shiny green tinged with bronze.

This is also a fairly late flowering azalea which avoids the late spring frost.

A. 'Orange Beauty'

The name gives an excellent description of the salmon-orange flowers. The leaves are quite large and covered in fine hairs, and in the autumn there is quite an impressive display of red and gold as the old leaves fall to be replaced again in the spring.

A. 'Palestrina'

White-flowered azaleas, massed together in a cool shady part of the garden, can give a magnificent spring display. 'Palestrina' is an old favourite but still one of the best white-flowered hybrids. It is very free-flowering with large white flowers which have faint green markings in the throat. It is definitely one of the more vigorous azaleas with a distinctly upright growing habit. It is perhaps one of the few that might need pruning from time to time in order to keep the plant bushy. In the autumn many of the large green leaves turn bright yellow giving an exciting splash of colour.

A. 'Rosebud'

'Rosebud' has a large distinctive flower which is a clear pink/red double. This is an excellent azalea for the small garden, and it can also be gently greenhouse forced to make an attractive spring pot plant.

A. 'Rose Greely'

Raised in America, 'Rose Greely' has two useful characteristics. Firstly, it is low-growing with a dense mass of quite large dark green leaves. Secondly, it has very large single white flowers which arrive late in the azalea season allowing you to extend the flowering season well into early summer.

A. 'Vuyk's Rosy Red'

Finally two excellent azaleas raised at the Vuyk van Nes nurseries in Holland. 'Rosy Red' has a low spreading habit sometimes up to 5 ft (1.5 m) wide. The flowers are large, light red with deep red markings in the throat.

A. 'Vuyk's Scarlet'

Really enormous deep red flowers with frilly edges, 'Vuyk's Scarlet' one of the very best compact azaleas for the small garden. It rarely exceeds 3 ft (90 cm) in height; therefore find a position quite near the front of the border.

Berberis

Here we have a genus of deciduous and evergreen shrubs which has produced a long list of outstanding garden shrubs; in fact there are few gardens without at least one. The following are just a few of the very best.

B. darwinii

Discovered in Chile in 1835 by Charles Darwin, this outstanding evergreen shrub produces a mass of glorious deep yellow flowers in spring which can often be followed in the autumn by a crop of blue berries. Happy on acid or alkaline soil and given fairly moist conditions, this shrub will thrive. Seed collected in autumn and sown immediately will generally germinate freely in the spring.

B. × ottawensis purpurea (Superba)

Certainly the best purple-leaved deciduous *Berberis*, strong growing with rich purple foliage. A fairly vigorous plant, it will eventually reach 5 – 6 ft (1.5 – 1.8 m) in height. Hard pruning in early spring will produce new growth with the best colour. Sometimes these purple foliage shrubs can appear rather sombre, but mixed with silver or yellow foliage they make a wonderful pattern. Summer cuttings in a propagator root quite easily.

B. 'Stapehill'

As yet a little known evergreen, but a *Berberis* that I have been very impressed with. Flowering

earlier than *B. darwinii*, an established bush will be covered every year in a mass of deep egg-yolk yellow flowers. It is also a great favourite with the bees, who return to the hive covered in bright yellow pollen. The only drawback with this magnificent *Berberis* is that it is very difficult to root, which perhaps answers the question of why it is not seen more often. Autumn-struck cuttings in a cold frame might be the answer.

B. stenophylla

Another old favourite, with graceful arching branches and rather paler yellow flowers appearing in late spring. As with all *Berberis*, this is a fairly prickly bush which forms a dense thicket. Hard pruning each year after flowering

Berberis 'Stapehill'

keeps the bush in good condition. Semi-ripe autumn cuttings root fairly well in a cold frame.

B. thunbergii

Among the *B. thunbergii* varieties, many are grown for their autumn colour and rich, rather juicy-looking, red berries.

B.t. atropurpurea

A useful, red-leaved deciduous *Berberis*, for general planting, which can be raised from seed.

B.t. 'Goldring'

This is a distinctive plant with purple leaves surrounded by a thin gold ring giving a definitely smart impression. It also has the welcome habit of all deciduous *Berberis* – a good autumn colour. Being a fairly recent introduction, propagation methods are not established, but try summer cuttings in a propagator.

B.t. 'Kelleris'

A green deciduous variety, in which young leaves are curiously mottled with cream. Fairly quick and easy to grow, a good spring pruning helps to produce the best coloured foliage. Where this unusual variety has appeared from is not clear, but seems to be a close relation of the pink mottled 'Rose Glow' – planted together they would make an interesting couple.

B.t. 'Little Favourite'

What a wonderful little shrub for mass planting, a really compact purple-leaved *Berberis* that will grow to at most 18 in (45 cm)! In one garden I spotted this *Berberis* planted alongside the golden-leaved *B.t. aurea*, and it really did make a wonderful combination. Unfortunately, this golden-leaved form is rather prone to sun scorch, so a sheltered site is best.

B.t. 'Rose Glow'

High in the popularity stakes is the unusual deciduous 'Rose Glow'. Leaves on the new growth are curiously mottled with silver and pink, making a really striking bush 5 – 6 ft (1.5 – 1.8 m) high. In autumn the leaves turn deep red. New young growth has the most pronounced variegation and this can best be encouraged by lightly pruning the bushes. Propagation from cuttings is not too easy; however soft cuttings taken in summer will root in a propagator.

B. valdiviana

It is surprising that this lovely *Berberis* has not become more popular. The sturdy evergreen bush has dark green evergreen leaves and really vicious thorns, and it would in fact make a very good, tough screening plant. The saffron yellow flowers hang in pendulous racemes like golden earrings. It can be propagated, though not easily, by means of semi-ripe cuttings. If the plant sets fruit new plants can also be raised from seed.

B. verruculosa and B. candidula

These two compact evergreens are closely related. They form compact bushes 4 – 6 ft (1.2 – 1.8 m) high, which after a few years form an almost impenetrable bush, with formidable thorns adding to the density. These are perhaps not the most exciting of the *Berberis* family, but both are useful as low screening. If planted as a hedge and clipped, they would form a tight barrier to keep anything out – or in! Flowers are pale yellow and appear in late spring. Propagate from autumn cuttings in a cold frame, or if a heated propagator is available late winter/early spring is a good time.

Buddleia (Butterfly Bush)

Common it may be, but there is something very nostalgic about buddleia. It conjures up visions of high summer and butterflies, and on warm days the sweet honey-like scent can be overwhelming. For a really tough plant that grows in almost any soil this one must take the prize. Hard pruning in

Berberis thunbergii 'Rose Glow'

spring is essential to encourage new strong growth and plenty of flowers. If you leave a buddleia it soon looks untidy. All buddleias are easy to root from semi-ripe summer cuttings, but as they have large soft leaves watch out for any fungal diseases while the cuttings are rooting. A routine 10-day spray with Benlate systemic fungicide will help control this problem.

B. davidii

The best of the *davidii* varieties are:
'Black Knight' – the darkest of all with deep purple flowers.
'Empire Blue' – a rich violet blue.
'Royal Red' – reddish purple.
'White Profusion' – large-flowered pure white.
The bright variegated form *B. davidii* 'Harlequin' with boldly variegated leaves and purple flowers makes an interesting combination.

B. alternifolia

This is a totally different plant; it retains the sweet buddleia smell, but forms a small weeping shrub or tree. I have seen really beautiful specimens growing as 8 – 10 ft (2.4 – 3 m) trees which are covered in summer in a mass of purple flowers.

Two new low-growing buddleias that may well become popular are *B.* 'Nanaho Blue' and *B.* 'Nanaho Purple'. For a small garden these are definitely worth looking out for.

Callistemon (Bottle Brush)

As a native of Australia, Bottle Brush is not too hardy, and can be damaged in a severe winter. The form *Callistemon citrinus* 'Splendens' is the most outstanding, with brilliant scarlet flowers all the summer. It can quite easily be grown from seed; the small seed pods appear to be dry and hard, and you must keep them in a warm dry place, preferably in an envelope or polythene bag, and the very fine seed will eventually appear. Sow in early spring.

Calluna

For cultivation details, see *Erica*.

C. vulgaris 'Alba Plena'

Growing to a height of around 8 – 12 in (20 – 30 cm), the dark green foliage provides an attractive foil for the double white flowers which appear in late summer.

C. v. 'Alportii'

Quite a tall growing *Calluna*, eventually achieving 18 – 24 in (45 – 60 cm). Flowering in late summer with single bright crimson flowers.

C. v. 'County Wicklow'

This is a really charming summer-flowering member of the genus. It is a low-growing, almost ground-hugging, plant with lovely soft pink double flowers which show up well against the dark green foliage. Usual height is 6 – 9 in (15 – 22 cm).

C. v. 'Elsie Purnell'

Silvery-green foliage, producing long spikes of lovely double pink flowers late in the summer. Height 18 – 20 in (45 – 50 cm).

C. v. 'Gold Haze'

The bright golden yellow foliage makes a lovely splash of contrast and colour through the summer. White flowers appear late in the season but can be rather insignificant among the bright foliage. Quite a compact *Calluna* 8 – 10 in (20 – 25 cm) in height.

C. v. 'Golden Feather'

As the name implies this is a fairly tall *Calluna* with plumes of soft yellow foliage tinged with orange. During the cold winter months the foliage turns to a deeper orange to red. Eventually *C. v.* 'Golden Feather' will grow to 24 in (60 cm).

C. v. 'H.E. Beale'

This is still one of the most popular and best late summer-flowering varieties. Quite a tall growing plant, 18 – 24 in (45 – 60 cm), with grey/green foliage, which produces spikes of lovely silver/pink flowers late in the summer and often well into the autumn. The foliage has a habit of turning brown in the winter but recovers again each spring.

C. v. 'Peter Sparkes'

This is very similar to 'H.E. Beale', but has deeper-coloured flowers.

C. v. 'Serlei'

Bright green foliage which becomes covered in single white flowers from late summer well into the autumn. Quite tall growing, around 24 in (60 cm).

C. v. 'Sunset'

This is a lovely winter foliage plant; the light green shoots are tipped with yellow and tinged red. A rather indifferent display of purple flowers can arrive during the late summer.

C. v. 'Tib'

A compact *Calluna* with dark green foliage. It is a valuable addition to the summer-flowering varieties, producing a profusion of double purple flowers from late summer well into the autumn.

Camellia

This is definitely one of the most exotic of all shrubs, and it has gained enormously in popularity over the past 20 – 30 years. The garden camellias are native to Asia, and included among the many exciting varieties is the exceptionally valuable plant *C. sinensis,* which covers many areas in India, Ceylon and Kenya. This of course is the Tea Plant, which has a typical shiny camellia leaf and in some varieties a single white flower.

For many years the camellia was treated as a tender plant and confined only to conservatories and frost-free countries, but in the past 30 – 40 years it has been realised that this is quite a hardy plant that can withstand many degrees of frost. Even now it is an exciting plant to grow under glass, where it requires no heat, and there is the enjoyment of the exotic flowers during late winter to very early spring. Apart from encouraging early flowers, the glass acts as protection against the spring frost and cold wind which can spoil the appearance of so many camellias in full flower.

Unfortunately, there are essential conditions to grow camellias successfully. The soil must be lime-free; if you live in an area of alkaline soil (containing lime) then you are restricted to growing these lovely plants in pots and tubs only, importing the necessary acid soil from outside.

For preference, camellias prefer a peaty soil, ideally in light shade, which helps to protect from the spring frost. A good acid loam with leafmould, peat or old bracken added will do equally well, however.

To see a magnificent camellia in full flower but badly frosted is a common and sad sight. To avoid this problem try to choose a protected site in your garden. Find a spot well sheltered from the early morning sun, as this combined with frost ruins so many beautiful flowers. The alternative is to use them as wall plants, choosing a west or north-west exposure. This will give you a greater chance of producing perfect flowers.

Camellias are certainly slow-growing, and for the first year or two they can be very shy with their flowers. The only advice here is patience, as once they develop into a reasonable bush you should have plenty of lovely flowers each year. Pruning will probably not be necessary, but can be done in spring or autumn if the bushes get out of hand.

Camellias are surprisingly disease and trouble free. One annoying pest that can occur under the leaves is the scale insect, which secretes a sticky honey dew onto the leaves, which then become covered in an unsightly sooty black mould. The best cure is to kill the scale with an insecticide containing Malathion, and wash the leaves with warm soapy water.

Most problems are due to poor planting

conditions. Leaves turning yellow may be an indication of lime in the soil or lack or nutrition. Each year a peat or bracken mulch will benefit camellias, as will a light dressing of fertilizer, 1 – 2 oz (30 – 60 g) per bush, depending on the size. Sulphate of ammonia, a quick-acting nitrogen feed, suits camellias very well.

After a very dry summer bud drop can occur, so if you are able to water and mulch in the summer this will all help.

Propagation from stem or leaf bud cuttings is quite easy using semi-ripe wood in the late summer. Make a very light wound, doing little more than removing the bark, as this will encourage rooting. Use rooting powder and insert the cutting in an open mixture of peat and sand. Bottom heat will help but is not essential.

By far the most free-flowering camellias are the *C. × williamsii* varieties, which result from a cross between the common *C. japonica* and a charming species called *C. saluenensis*, an evergreen shrub up to 15 ft (4.5 m) high. *C. japonica* varieties have the easily recognised round glossy green leaves forming a dense evergreen bush, and they are sometimes shy to flower for the first 2 – 3 years. The *C. williamsii* varieties on the other hand flower with great freedom, almost from the cutting stage onwards. A very young plant can often set too many buds which should be thinned out to encourage more growth.

C. cuspidata × saluenensis ('Cornish Snow')

It could be said that the common *C. japonica* lacks individual character from one plant to the next, although there is a variety of flower shapes and colours ranging from white and pink to red – but exotic and exciting as they are there is a certain uniform character about many camellias. This delicate hybrid, raised in Cornwall, is a very obvious individual. It can grow into a fairly open shrub of about 6 ft (2 m) in height. With narrow strap-like leaves, it produces each year quite early in the spring a mass of quite small single flowers with a central bunch of yellow stamens. When well established the plant is quite vigorous and needs to be lightly pruned after flowering to keep a compact shape.

C. japonica

C. j. 'Adolphe Audusson'

This is by no means a new camellia, but it is still one of the best double red varieties with conspicuous yellow stamens. This is generally a slow-growing genus of shrubs, but 'Adolphe Adusson', with a rather upright habit, is certainly one of the most vigorous. The foliage is exceptionally glossy.

C. j. 'Alba Simplex'

'Alba Simplex' has, as the name implies, a very simple white flower with a pronounced central cluster of yellow stamens. All white camellias are prone to early frost damage which marks the white petals, so a sheltered site should be chosen. This popular old camellia can grow up to 20 ft (6 m) high.

C. j. 'Carter's Sunburst'

Many new camellias have been raised in the USA, with exceptionally beautiful flowers. 'Carter's Sunburst' has very large semi-double flowers which are primarily white with light and dark pink stripes. It makes a very compact shrub.

C. j. 'C.M. Wilson'

Another camellia raised in the USA, with enormous flowers up to 5 or 6 in (12 – 15 cm) across. These very large flowering camellias are exceptionally beautiful, but bad weather can ruin the flowers. Unless you have very favourable spring weather, confine this camellia to a conservatory.

C. j. 'Drama Girl'

This camellia has enormous, semi-double, pale pink flowers, which are so large and heavy that they have a slightly drooping habit. It is another candidate for the greenhouse or conservatory.

C. j. 'Elegans'

Sometimes called 'Chandleri Elegans', this camellia was raised many years ago and over the years has won many awards for excellence. When not in flower this shrub can be recognised by the spreading, almost weeping habit. It has deep, rosy-pink flowers, sometimes flecked with white.

C.j. 'Jupiter'

The flowers, which always appear to be very alert, are scarlet, sometimes with small patches of white, with a very bold central bunch of gold stamens.

C.j. 'Lady Vansittart'

This is one of the bushiest of all camellias, with distinctive, slightly curled leaves, which are narrow and pointed. The fairly small neat flowers are semi-double, and white with rose stripes. Sometimes on the same bush almost white flowers and all pink flowers are seen mixed with the striped ones.

C. j. 'Leonard Messel'

This is a distinctive camellia that has been raised by crossing the very large flowered C. reticulata with the smaller free-flowering C. × williamsii. The result is a plant that has the large pink flowers of C. reticulata plus the hardiness of C. × williamsii. The leaves are narrow and grey-green, and it grows into a fairly open bush. This lovely plant is perhaps one of the last to flower, carrying on well into late spring.

C. j. 'Magnoliiflora'

The small star-like flowers are very attractive on this compact camellia. Masses of semi-double soft pink flowers are produced in profusion all over the bush.

C.j. 'Preston Rose'

The shape of this flower is usually described as 'paeony form' and it appears as a mass of petals very similar to a carnation. The flowers are deep pink on this fairly vigorous upright bush.

C. reticulata

For a cool conservatory C. reticulata and its various clones can be very exciting. In mild climates it will certainly thrive outside in a sheltered position. It forms a vigorous tree, as opposed to bush, up to 30 ft (10 m) high, with grey-green, rather narrow leaves. It has enormous, very showy, deep pink flowers 3 – 4 in (7 – 10 cm) across, of rather irregular shape as if made of many layers of pink tissue paper.

C. sasanqua

Its native home is Japan, where apparently this is an exceptionally popular camellia. Why this is not grown more often elsewhere is a mystery, because it has the remarkable advantage of flowering late in the autumn and often well into winter. This is a camellia that is as hardy as C. japonica, but flowering so late in the year the flowers can be very vulnerable to weather damage. If you therefore have a sheltered sunny wall or fence, try growing this lovely autumn/winter-flowering camellia. Most C. sasanqua camellias have large and small forms, the colours ranging from white and pale pink to deep purplish-red.

The varieties have some fairly difficult names, like the white flowered with pink edges of 'Narumi-Gata', or the similar coloured 'Fukuzo-Tsumi'. There are other simpler names such as the single 'Plantation Pink'; another rather lovely double pink from the USA is 'Jean May' and a pink and white flower is called 'Rainbow'.

C × williamsii

A cross carried out between two species C. japonica and C. saluenensis has over the years produced a whole range of hardy free-flowering varieties which have done more than anything else to make this one of the most popular garden shrubs today. One great asset of the C. × williamsii forms is that they start to flower at a very early age – in fact sometimes they flower rather too soon, producing a mass of buds on

12 in (30 cm) high youngsters: if this should happen the majority of buds are best gently removed to allow the plant to grow. One way to recognise the majority of *C. × williamsii* camellias is by the narrow-pointed leaves which can be quite dull, as opposed to the glossy round leaves of the *japonica* forms.

C. × w. 'Anticipation'

'Anticipation', a native of New Zealand, has a very upright habit of growth, making it ideal for a narrow site. The flowers are very large and described as 'paeony form', indicating a double effect very similar to that of carnation flowers. The upright habit also makes this an excellent variety to plant against a wall.

C. × w. 'Brigadoon'

This has exceptionally large rose pink flowers on a dense compact bush. The size of the glorious pink flowers certainly makes 'Brigadoon' worth growing.

C. × w. 'China Clay'

White camellia flowers are extremely attractive against the glossy green foliage. Unfortunately, however, white does show up any weather or frost damage; therefore a sheltered site is important if you want unblemished flowers. 'China Clay' has double white flowers and excellent foliage with a rather open habit of growth.

C. × w. 'Debbie'

This is another native of New Zealand and one of the fastest-growing of all camellias, often exceeding 12 – 18 in (30 – 45 cm) each year. It has upright, slightly untidy habit, and of all the *C. × williamsii* camellias it can be rather shy to produce many flowers in the first year or two. Attractive clear pink semi-double flowers.

C. × w. 'Donation'

This is probably one of the most popular

Càmellia × williamsii 'Debbie'

camellias. To see a large specimen bush smothered in semi-double orchid pink flowers certainly justifies all the praise and awards that have been heaped on 'Donation'. It is exceptionally free-flowering, in fact it is almost too keen to flower when only 12 in (30 cm) high. Make sure that your new plant does not flower too profusely for the first year or so – brace yourself to remove an excess of flower buds in early spring and you will then have a fairly quick-growing evergreen shrub. With distinctive narrow grey-green leaves, once established you can almost guarantee a wonderful display every spring.

Camellia × williamsii 'Donation'

C. × w. 'Elsie Jury'

If you want to extend the flowering season this is another hybrid from New Zealand that is one of the last to flower, extending the main spring flowering season. It has very large double pale pink flowers with good bold foliage. One criticism of this lovely plant is that because the flowers are so large and heavy they have a tendency to hang downwards and therefore do not display themselves very well.

C. × w. 'Francis Hanger'

This free-flowering upright bush makes an excellent wall plant. It has simple white flowers with a pronounced bunch of yellow stamens in the centre. The leaves of 'Francis Hanger' have a definite curl, making this a distinctive plant.

Camellia × williamsii 'Mary Christian'

C. × w. 'J.C. Williams'

Exceptionally free-flowering, this is one of the very first *C. × williamsii* camellias to be raised. The flowers are single white with a flush of pink. Perhaps the single flowers are rather more delicate and therefore require careful placing in the garden to avoid winter damage.

C. × w. 'Mary Christian'

This is a vigorous single pink-flowered camellia. It is one of the first to flower, often showing colour

Carpenteria californica

in late winter. Establish a large bush and you can enjoy the luxury of picking sprigs of this lovely plant for early spring flower arrangements.

Carpenteria

What a spectacular shrub *C. californica* is! It is a native of California and really needs a mild climate or certainly a warm wall to grow against. The fragrant 2 – 3 in (5 – 7.5 cm) wide flowers appear in summer; pure white in colour with a pronounced bunch of yellow stamens in the middle, they make a strong contrast with the dark green evergreen foliage. It is not a common plant – apart from anything else it is difficult to propagate. Cuttings taken in summer will sometimes root, but are not at all easy.

Caryopteris

A very useful shrub for late summer flowers, *C. × clandonensis* has silver grey foliage showing off the delightful powder-blue flowers. There are a number of forms, of which *C. × c.* 'Heavenly Blue' is the best. Semi-ripe cuttings taken in summer will root very easily.

Ceanothus

Native to the Pacific coast of the USA, this fast-growing range of deciduous and evergreen shrubs makes a great contribution to the garden. Unfortunately they are fairly tender, but with such rapid growth they are always worth replacing. Nearly all the best garden varieties have varying shades of bright blue flowers in rather distinctive, round, puff ball shapes. Apart from making excellent free-growing shrubs, *Ceanothus* are ideal wall plants and benefit greatly from the protection of a sunny wall. The following are well worth trying.

C. arboreus 'Trewithen Blue'

Sadly this is one of the most tender, originating from the lovely Trewithen Gardens in Cornwall.

Ceanothus arboreus 'Trewithen Blue'

In fact, under ideal conditions, this *Ceanothus* can almost make a small tree. If you have a warm corner it is worth trying. It will root from semi-ripe summer cuttings, but is not too easy.

C. arboreus 'Yankee Point'

This is a relatively new *Ceanothus*, which can be grown as an unsupported shrub or trained against the wall. It is a fairly vigorous shrub producing a mass of glossy green foliage and powder-blue flower heads in the spring. Even out of flower the good foliage makes this an interesting plant. Summer cuttings root fairly easily.

C. 'Autumnal Blue'

The great joy of this family is the long flowering period. 'Autumnal Blue' is reasonably hardy and flowers late summer to early autumn. Take semi-ripe summer cuttings to propagate.

C. 'Blue Mound'

This is a useful new variety originating from Hilliers' Nursery at Winchester, England. It can be described as one of the ground-cover *Ceanothus*, and will form a dense mound about 2 ft (60 cm) high. Each spring it is covered in a mass of pale blue flowers. It appears to be fairly hardy. Propagate from semi-ripe cuttings in summer.

C. 'Burkwoodii'

Again this is a useful shrub as it flowers late, filling a late summer to early autumn gap. The flowers are dark blue in colour. Semi-ripe summer cuttings root fairly easily.

C. 'Cascade'

This is an absolute winner! A well-grown shrub of 'Cascade' is certainly a picture. The habit of this shrub, as the name implies, is a dense weeping bush. Once established, it is very free-flowering with the brightest blue flowers. As a very vigorous grower it does need annual pruning after

flowering to keep it in shape. It is perhaps on the tender side, but so quick to grow that it is always worth replacing. Cuttings in summer will root, but not easily, and they are liable to die when you transplant rooted cuttings to a small pot.

C. dentatus

This is perhaps one of the most popular *Ceanothus* and it is very useful as a wall shrub. It has very distinctive small round shiny green leaves, and if pruned each year will make a dense evergreen mat against the wall with clusters of powder blue flowers in late spring/early summer. As with many fast-growing shrubs their lifespan can be fairly short, and it is probably fair to say that many *Ceanothus*, after a number of years, will suddenly die for no apparent reason. Semi-ripe summer cuttings will root fairly easily in a propagator; keep a spare plant handy for replacement.

C. 'Gloire de Versailles'

The best known of the deciduous *Ceanothus*. The very deep blue *C.* 'Henri Desfosse' and pink flowered *C.* 'Perle Rose' are not quite so common. These are useful shrubs as they flower late in the summer through to early autumn with a mass of pale blue flowers. Fairly constant pruning is essential; otherwise you develop a rather ugly and untidy bush. Prune in the spring to form a compact plant. This variety will root fairly easily from summer cuttings.

Ceratostigma

C. willmottianum is a low-growing deciduous shrub which was collected in China by the great plant hunter Ernest Henry Wilson. The attraction of this shrub is the late flowering period, starting in summer and going on until mid-autumn. Definitely a sun lover, it can unfortunately be damaged in a cold winter, but generally sprouts again from the base. It is easily rooted from summer cuttings.

Chaenomeles

This is a range of lovely shrubs, native to China and Japan. To many, this range of shrubs is still known as 'Japonica'. No doubt this has arisen from one of the earliest species of *C. japonica* introduced into Great Britain around 1869. It is unfortunate that this excellent genus of plants does not possess a more simple name. Completely hardy and thriving in most soils, it makes a useful free-growing shrub and an excellent wall plant, and if well trimmed will form an interesting hedge. One of the joys of this plant is the fact that flowers appear from fat round buds so early in the spring. The large simple flowers are mainly scarlet to orange-flame, but white and pink varieties are also available.

To get the best from your wall plants, annual pruning after flowering is essential; long shoots should be cut back to short spurs. Being related to the quince, a large crop of fruit can be produced, which reputedly makes excellent jelly. It is fairly easy to propagate from soft to semi-ripe summer cuttings. Rooted cuttings should not be potted on until the following spring.

C. speciosa 'Moerloosii'

An interesting combination of pink and white flowers.

C. speciosa 'Nivalis'

Pure white flowers. A shrub to brighten a dark corner.

C. × superba 'Crimson and Gold'

Very popular and free-flowering with bright crimson petals and golden anthers.

C. × superba 'Knap Hill Scarlet'

The large simple flowers are a lovely shade of deep orange. Cut a few sprigs in spring just as the buds begin to swell and you can enjoy the rich-coloured flowers indoors.

C. × superba 'Pink Lady'

Large clear pink flowers with a fairly low spreading habit – certainly an excellent free-flowering variety. Summer cuttings root fairly easily.

Chimonanthus

Almost any shrub that will produce winter flowers *and* a delicious scent is worth growing. Fairly tolerant of most soils, *C. praecox* 'Grandiflorus' prefers the shelter of a sunny wall. The delicate pale yellow flowers come as a great surprise in mid-winter and appear undaunted by even the most extreme weather. This is a fairly variable shrub with forms that flower profusely, whereas others grow happily and produce few flowers. Short sprigs picked just before flowering are lovely in the house. If you find a good flowering

Chimonanthus praecox 'Grandiflorus'

form it will root from semi-ripe cuttings. Seed is also possible but could be the cause of many poor flowering forms.

Cistus

As natives of Spain and Portugal, this genus of shrubs will thrive under the most extreme dry weather; in their homeland they grow in dry rocky hills which may not see rain for many months. Unfortunately, a number are not too hardy and will be damaged during very cold winters. A light covering of bracken over the plant will do a lot to prevent frost damage. Apart from being very attractive shrubs producing a mass of flowers through the summer *Cistus* also have the great advantage of growing on dry hot banks in fairly poor soil. They are all fairly quick-growing and need severe pruning after flowering; if left the shrub does become very lanky and ugly.

C. 'Blanche'

With the flowers set against the dark green foliage this is a beautiful plant but unfortunately it is not too hardy. Summer cuttings root fairly easily.

C. × corbariensis

This is one of the hardiest in the genus and it makes a compact shrub around 3 ft (90 cm) high and 3 ft wide. Pink-tipped buds open to single white flowers with a yellow flush at the base. A well-established plant, if placed in full sun, a requirement of all *Cistus*, will give a consistently good display every summer. It is easy to root from summer cuttings.

C. × purpureus

Very aromatic leaves are characteristic of this genus and clearly identifies them as plants of the hot dry Mediterranean hills. *C. × purpureus* has grey-green foliage and beautiful deep pink flowers with a conspicuous blotch in the base. In colder

Cistus × purpureus

64

Cistus 'Silver Pink'

areas this species will need a well-sheltered position.

C. 'Silver Pink'

A neat bush growing to a height of 2 – 3 ft (60 – 90 cm) with large papery flowers which are clear pink with a bunch of yellow stamens in the centre. This is a fairly hardy variety and summer cuttings are the best means of propagation.

C. × skanbergii

Forming a low hummock this is apparently a natural hybrid collected in Greece. It is a charming shrub with small, very delicate, pink flowers.

Convolvulus

Any mention of the name *Convolvulus* conjures up visions of 'bindweed', a really pernicious garden weed. *C. cneorum*, however, is a well-behaved and striking member of the same genus. It is a fairly low-growing compact plant not exceeding 2 – 2½ ft (60 – 75 cm) when fully grown, with leaves covered in fine silky hairs which give an overall sparkling silver effect. During the summer months the large trumpet flowers, which are white tinged with pink, open in succession. It is a shrub that requires full sun and, being somewhat tender, the shelter of a warm wall. To keep a good shape light pruning each spring will help. *C. cneorum* will root easily from summer cuttings.

Cornus (Dogwood)

Here is a collection of shrubs offering something all the year round; foliage and flowers in the

Cornus florida rubra

spring and early summer, including a number of slow-growing aristocrats of the shrub world; then in winter you can enjoy the lovely red and yellow-green bark of *C. alba* varieties. As a further bonus, *Cornus* makes a charming ground cover plant for acid soils.

C. alba varieties are tolerant of most soils and have the advantage of thriving in fairly damp boggy conditions; therefore they can be used around ponds and marshland. To get the best from them, a good hard prune is essential *every* year, and early in the cycle.

C. alba 'Sibirica' (Westonbirt Dogwood)

This is the best of the red-stemmed varieties. Keep pruning each year and you will produce a clump of brilliant red stems throughout the year.

C. canadensis (Creeping Dogwood)

This is really a herbaceous species, but is well worth a mention. It will only grow in soils that are free of lime, and under ideal woodland conditions it will form a dense carpet with distinctive small white dogwood flowers in spring followed by autumn berries. It can be propagated from runners.

C. florida rubra (Flowering Dogwood)

A native of the eastern USA, this lovely shrub is none too common. Sadly it is not an easy plant either to propagate or to grow. The growing requirements are rich well drained loam and a fairly sheltered position. The deep pink flowers or bracts open during early summer and are often damaged by late spring frost.

C. kousa chinensis

From China and Japan, this shrub can eventually

Cornus kousa chinensis

Cornus stolonifera 'Flaviramea'

make a very large bush, at least 10 ft (3 m) high. In early summer the weeping branches are covered in distinctive flowers or bracts (the true flower is bunched in the centre and surrounded by four bracts) which stand up all along the stem. The long-lasting flowers are a distinctive creamy white with a deep purple centre. It is unfortunately fairly slow-growing. Nevertheless, they say that all the best things are worth waiting for and this certainly applies to *C. k. chinensis*. An added bonus in some years is a show of brilliant autumn colour as the leaves fall.

C. mas (Cornelian Cherry)

The rather more flamboyant winter flowering Witch Hazels may have eclipsed the delicate winter-flowering *Cornus mas*, but any shrub that flowers in late winter is worth planting if you have the space, and this is a fairly vigorous shrub or small tree. It is a delicate and charming winter shrub, on which the bare stems are covered in a mass of soft yellow tufted flowers. It can be grown from seed.

C. stolonifera 'Flaviramea'

Plant a clump of this alongside the brilliant red Westonbirt! Here we have contrasting bright yellow stems adding useful winter colour. It is the fresh young shoots that have the best colour, so prune hard early in the year. Both 'Flaviramea' and Westonbirt will root readily from summer cuttings.

Corylopsis

This is a charming group of early spring-flowering shrubs closely related to the hazel, as well as the winter-flowering witch hazels. All the flowers are soft yellow and appear in early spring. Unfortunately such early flowers are susceptible to spring frosts; therefore a light woodland situation affording some shelter is ideal. This genus does not like chalky soils.

C. pauciflora

This is a very delicate shrub, eventually reaching

Corylopsis willmottiae

4 – 6 ft (1.2 – 1.8 m) making a dense twiggy little bush. Once established, a mass of soft primrose yellow flowers appear in early spring, which have a distinctive scent similar to cowslips. Late spring frosts can so often spoil this shrub. So try to find a lightly shaded part of the garden and add plenty of peat. Soft summer cuttings will root in gentle heat; rooted cuttings should be potted in the following spring.

C. willmottiae

Here we have a taller shrub growing up to 12 ft (3.6 m), the young shoots being light bronze. Flowers are soft greenish-yellow with a distinct fresh scent. Again this is a shrub that does not like chalky soil and which thrives in peaty, light woodland.

Cotinus coggyria

Corylus (Hazel)

Apart from the hazels which are planted for their nuts, there are a number that have value as garden shrubs. All grow strongly on loamy soil and are very suitable for chalky areas.

C. avellana 'Contorta' (Corkscrew Hazel)

If you like shrubs with curiously twisted stems then the aptly-named Corkscrew Hazel is the best. This curious plant was discovered around 1863 growing in a Gloucestershire hedgerow. The strangely twisted stems produce a fine display of catkins in late winter, giving a fairly striking effect.

Corylus avellana 'Contorta'

In spring and summer the large hazel leaves almost disguise the twisted effect. This plant can be rooted from soft summer cuttings, and if you are successful do not pot on until the spring.

C. maxima 'Purpurea' (Purple Leaf Filbert)

This is a useful member of the hazel family, with deep purple leaves, for screening or background planting. Hard pruning in the spring encourages the best coloured young shoots. Propagation from cuttings in the summer is not easy and they often die during the first winter.

Cotinus (Venetian Sumach or Smoke Tree)

Here is a group of deciduous shrubs growing up to 15 ft (4.5 m) high, forming a spreading bush. Primarily planted for their deep red spring and summer foliage, this genus also gives excellent autumn colour. The fluffy bunches of flowers

71

arrive in mid-summer and start off resembling deep pink smoke; this eventually turns grey, creating a lovely overall effect and accounting for the name 'Smoke Tree'.

C. coggygria

This green-leaved form looks stunning covered in the soft smoky flowers and possibly gives the best autumn colour.

C. c. 'Foliis Purpureis' "Notcutts Variety"

Apart from an exceptionally difficult name, this is one of the deepest purple, almost black, garden shrubs, offering a marvellous contrast with silver foliage. Under fairly poor soil conditions plenty of flowers will appear in summer to give the beautiful 'smoky' effect. This plant will root from soft summer cuttings, but it is not easy.

Cotoneaster

Spring flowers, autumn berries, ground cover, screening, and one excellent wall shrub! Generally it is fair to say that cotoneasters do not produce outstanding spring flowers, generally small and white with a hint of pink. Some of the low-growing varieties, especially *C. conspicuus Decorus*, are much favoured by bees. The brilliant red and yellow berries are the main attraction for garden planting, but unfortunately the berries are also popular with the birds. The low ground cover forms do have a limited garden use and can act as useful labour-saving plants, but their main value is for urban planting of highway roundabouts, housing estate borders and similar. All cotoneasters are fairly easy to root from summer cuttings and some will grow from seed.

C. 'Cornubia'

This is the giant of the cotoneaster genus, growing up to 20 ft (6 m). In autumn these shrubs are a wonderful sight, covered in bunches of brilliant scarlet berries.

C. dammeri

Here is a shrub that appears determined to hug the earth as closely as possible; consequently it forms a very effective ground cover. As with many prostrate shrubs, this useful cotoneaster was discovered in China at an altitude of around 7000 ft (2000 m), where years of wind and wild weather have taught these plants that near to the earth is the most favourable place to be. Being evergreen, this is another useful plant for extensive ground cover. The small white flowers in spring are followed by a crop of red berries. Under ideal conditions it can be very vigorous, rooting where it touches the ground, and it may end up covering more than you require. It is easily propagated from cuttings, or rooted layers from existing plants.

C. 'Exburiensis'

This large cotoneaster is most useful for background screening in the smaller garden. A good crop of the yellow berries will remain well into the autumn. It can be propagated from summer cuttings.

C. horizontalis (The Fish Tail Cotoneaster)

This is possibly the most attractive of the low-growing cotoneasters, with numerous bright green leaves remaining on the bush well into autumn. Eventually they turn scarlet and orange, finally falling to reveal a mass of red berries. The bare branches reveal the curious fish bone structure of this plant – hence its common name. As a shrub to grow up a house wall or fence this must be one of the best, irrespective of aspect. Also as a labour-saving ground-cover plant it is very useful indeed, and scores over many other ground-cover cotoneasters in having such attractive, dark glossy foliage. There is also a variegated form *C. h.* 'Variegatus' which is perhaps not so vigorous. *C. horizontalis* can be grown from seed or summer cuttings.

Cotoneaster 'Cornubia'

C. 'Hybridus Pendulus'

Usually grown as a small weeping shrub or tree on a clear 6 ft (1.8 m) stem, this is a lovely cotoneaster which develops a cascade of weeping branches covered each autumn in brilliant red berries. Birds will have a go at the berries when cold weather arrives, but a spray with a proprietary bird repellent does no harm to the birds and will keep them off a little longer. It can be rooted fairly easily from summer cuttings.

C. 'Rothschildianus'

A large shrub with yellow berries lasting well into the autumn, which can be propagated by means of summer cuttings.

Cytisus (Broom)

Here we have some exceptionally free-flowering members of the legume family. After flowering it is essential to prune all brooms, for they are quick-growing and if left untended soon form an untidy, heavy bush. Generally, brooms have a fairly short life and will need replanting every five or six years to achieve the best results.

The majority will root easily from summer cuttings, with the exception of *C. battandieri* which is very difficult – seed is no doubt the best method here. All brooms thrive in full sun and prefer light sandy soil.

C. battandieri (Moroccan Broom)

This is a quick-growing shrub with fine silver foliage and large masses of yellow flowers smelling of pineapple. It is surprisingly hardy and quick-growing, and in order to keep a good shape an annual prune after flowering is essential. It can be grown as a free-standing shrub but it is seen at its best trained against a warm wall. It is a surprisingly difficult plant to root from cuttings, although after a hot summer it will set seed which germinates quite readily

C. × kewensis

This is a charming species with a low spreading habit rarely achieving more than 12 in (30 cm) in height, but often 5 – 6 ft (1.5 – 1.8 m) across. In late spring it has a mass of soft yellow flowers, and is ideal for growing over a wall or for rock garden planting. I remember seeing a marvellous combination of *C. × kewensis* underplanted with a mass of *Gentiana acaulis*; the intense blue gentian flowers combined very well with the soft yellow broom. This is not a common plant; when offered for sale in a pot it may look unexciting, but in an open sunny position it can be very rewarding.

C. praecox (Warminster Broom)

With a mass of tumbling pale yellow flowers this broom is rather more delicate than the *C. scoparius* hybrids, and is an easy-going plant included in so many spring gardens. There is an attractive white form *C. × p.* 'Albus', and a deeper yellow one of Dutch origin, *C. × p.* 'Allgold'. As with all of this genus, pruning after flowering is essential. Plants five to six years old tend to become rather gaunt and are best dug out and replaced. It is quite easy to root from summer cuttings.

C. scoparius

This is not exactly a garden shrub, in fact it is more a weed, but when seen in a mass of bright yellow flowers it can be very attractive. The best of the *C. scoparius* hybrids include the following.
C. s. 'Andreanus' – yellow and rich crimson.
C. s. 'Burkwoodii' – maroon flowers with yellow wings.
C. s. 'Cornish Cream' – ivory cream flowers with yellow wings.
C. s. 'Golden Sunlight' – rich yellow flowers.
C. s. 'Windlesham Ruby' – dark mahogany crimson flowers.
C. s. 'Zeelandia' – lilac and cream flowers.

Daboecia

This is a charming genus of low-growing shrubs, closely allied to *Calluna* and *Erica*. It is a native of Western Europe and Ireland, where it can be found growing wild. Planted in large clumps it forms excellent ground cover and has the added advantage of a long flowering season, from early summer to mid-autumn. To keep neat and free flowering prune lightly in early spring. All *Daboecia* will root from summer cuttings.

D. cantabrica 'Alba'

This low shrub will eventually grow to about 2 ft (60 cm) in height. The flowers are quite large and bell-shaped. It is an excellent subject to plant among other taller plants. *D. c.* 'Alba', as the name implies, has simple white flowers.

D. cantabrica 'Atropurpurea'

The flowers are rich red-purple, which mixes in well with the other varieties.

D. cantabrica 'Bicolor'

This is a very pretty plant, with some flowers white, and some purple and others combining both colours, all on the same plant.

Daphne

There is a curious mystique about this genus. They are definitely plants which require individual attention, unlike the forsythia type of shrub that thrives and flourishes almost anywhere. For this reason they are a challenge, and if successful you have an exciting and rewarding plant. A rich, well-drained loam and an open, sunny position are essential requirements. They are generally difficult to propagate from cuttings; however one or two set seed that germinates fairly well.

D. bholua 'Gurkha'

This is one of the semi-evergreen varieties that may need the protection of a south wall in the cooler localities. The scented flowers are in clusters of pale mauve and white and can start appearing from late winter until early spring. This is an exciting new introduction which is at present

Daphne bholua 'Gurkha'

very scarce. Propagation is difficult; the early plants I have seen have been grafted.

Daphne × burkwoodii

Try to obtain the clone 'Somerset'. This is a delightful, low evergreen shrub, not too easy to grow, which will form a bush about 2 ft (60 cm) high which is covered in a mass of pale pink flowers during early summer. It is not easy to root from cuttings.

D. cneorum

This is another little treasure! In spring this low-growing *Daphne* is a mass of deep pink flowers. It is not an easy one to propagate, but you can root soft cuttings. If you succeed, transplant with great care into a small pot in a good loamy compost with no fertilizer.

D. mezereum

This early spring-flowering *Daphne* is perhaps one of the easiest to grow, happy in both alkaline and acid soils. At one time this was a common plant in cottage gardens, but over the years it has become more scarce. Virus disease may account for the disappearance.

The typical purple-pink, richly-scented flowers appear on the bare stems. Seed is the best method of propagation; the bright red poisonous fruits appear soon after flowering, and if you can keep the birds at bay sow immediately in sharp sand, leaving the pots or boxes outside to overwinter. Then bring them into a cool glasshouse in early spring and you should usually achieve quite good germination. From a batch of seedlings you can get a fairly deep red form and a white-flowered form.

As temperamental as all *Daphne* species, *D. mezereum* can thrive for many years and then die for no apparent reason – so keep a seedling or two on hand.

D. odora 'Aureomarginata'

This is an unusual variety with creamy white leaf margins. It forms a well-rounded evergreen shrub about 3 ft (90 cm) high, the distinctive pink to purple scented flowers appearing in late winter to early spring. An attractive evergreen, it is fairly easy to grow, but sometimes a little light trimming helps to keep the bush in good shape. It is wise to give this shrub a site well away from the cold north wind. This is one variety of *Daphne* that will root fairly easily from late summer cuttings.

Deutzia

Deutzias are easy-going shrubs that thrive in nearly all soils; the main requirements are for an open sunny site and plenty of space to develop. Quick-growing, established plants will give a guaranteed display of pink or white flowers. The only other requirement to keep the shrub in good condition is to cut old wood right back to the base

Deutzia × elegantissima 'Rosalind'

soon after flowering. All *Deutzia* are eas propagate from cuttings.

D. × elegantissima 'Rosalind'

This deep pink *Deutzia* is perhaps not the sturdiest grower in this genus but it is certainly one of the most attractive.

D. longifolia 'Veitchii'

This is a strong growing shrub reaching 4 – 6 ft (1.2 – 1.8 m) in height. The double flowers are soft lavender in colour and appear in early summer.

D. 'Magicien'

A rather attractive purple streak on the reverse of this *Deutzia* makes it well worth planting. Another fairly similar hybrid is 'Contraste' with equally attractive marked flowers. All *Deutzia* flower very freely, and if pruned annually form attractive mounds of early summer colour. *D.* 'Magicien' is very easy to propagate from semi-ripe cuttings.

D. × rosea 'Carminea'

One of the more compact and graceful *Deutzia* for the smaller garden where space is at a premium this is one of the best. It is covered in a mass of rose carmine flowers during late spring.

Elaeagnus

This genus provides a range of very useful hardy evergreen shrubs which are of great value in the garden. Happy in full sun or semi-shade, they are not too fussy about the type of soil. Three of the *Elaeagnus* have gold variegations on their leaves which makes them very popular evergreens for the flower arranger. As screening plants or hedges they make an invaluable contribution to the garden.

E. ebbingei

Perhaps not the most exciting plant, but *E.*

Elaeagnus 'Gilt Edge'

ebbingei is extremely tough, forming an excellent evergreen screen or hedge, eventually growing to around 15 ft (4.5 m) in height. The silvery leaves are covered in a curious white dust giving a texture similar to sandpaper. A mass of rather insignificant white but scented flowers appear in autumn and these are followed by small pale orange fruits covered in the same white dust. This is probably one of the fastest-growing *Elaeagnus* and needs constant summer pruning to keep the bush or hedge under control. Propagation is by late summer cuttings.

E. 'Gilt Edge'

This variety definitely has the brightest evergreen foliage of all, bright yellow leaves with just a hint of green. It is a shrub that has a rather weak constitution and may take a year or two to establish. Not vigorous or very tall growing, when seen at its best the foliage can be very beautiful. Cuttings are not so easy, but they will root; however care must be taken to nurse the plants in their first year or so.

E. 'Limelight'

Again a fairly vigorous variety of *Elaeagnus*, this is a fairly recent introduction that will become more popular. The quite large leathery leaves have attractive, fairly soft variegation combining shades of gold, olive, pale and dark green. Unfortunately, one apparent disadvantage is that the foliage has a tendency to revert and shoots of plain green leaves, closely resembling its relation *E. ebbingei*, often occur. These shoots should always be cut out with secateurs, leaving space and light for the variegated foliage. This plant has an upright habit and flowers freely in late autumn. Propagation is by late summer cuttings.

E. 'Maculata Aurea'

Possibly one of the most widely planted variegated shrubs, this bold evergreen has a shiny gold splash in the middle of each leaf. The bright foliage is excellent for indoor decoration, especially during the dull days of winter. Apart from growing as a free shrub this *Elaeagnus* makes an excellent hedge; prune during the summer months. Cuttings taken late summer to early autumn will root fairly easily.

Embothrium (Chilean Fire Bush)

This is a spectacular shrub that sadly will not tolerate any lime in the soil and is not too hardy. Under ideal open but sheltered conditions this evergreen shrub or small tree produces a mass of brilliant scarlet flowers in early summer, giving a display of colour long after many of the spring flowering shrubs have finished. This plant is definitely fussy, but given well-drained rich soil and plenty of moisture it will thrive. If seed is available it will germinate, and summer cuttings will root if given great care. Make sure that you take cuttings from a free-flowering bush as there are some very shy flower forms available.

Enkianthus

Best suited to light woodland conditions, *E. campanulatus* is another shrub that will not tolerate lime. Growing to around 6 ft (1.8 m) in

Embothrium coccineum

height, the whole plant is covered in a mass of small lily-of-the-valley shaped flowers during late spring. In autumn all the *Enkianthus* put on a spectacular display of crimson and yellow autumn colours. Seed is probably the easiest way to propagate this deciduous shrub.

Erica

Apart from the rose, I doubt if there is any plant that has produced such a profusion of new varieties as the heather group, *Erica* and *Calluna* (see p. 52). There are heathers in foliage or flower that can give colour all year round. Green, grey, yellow, gold, bronze, red and copper foliage produces a magnificent patchwork, with flowers of varying shades of pink, white, red and purple.

The native habitat of heathers which grow wild in temperate climates such as Great Britain gives some clues as to their garden requirements. Firstly, they always grow in full sun; if planted in

Enkianthus campanulatus

the shade they become tall and straggly. Secondly, they often grow on peaty moorland, and apart from a few exceptions will not tolerate lime in the soil. The exceptions are the winter-flowering varieties such as *E. carnea* 'King George' and *E.c.* 'Springwood White', as well as a number of the tree heathers such as *E. arborea* (the wild Mediterranean tree heather), *E. lusitanica* (the Portuguese heather) and *E. terminalis* (the Corsican heather).

The optimum soil conditions for a good heather garden are found in areas of light sandy loam, into which should ideally be incorporated good quantities of moss peat. Fertiliser should be kept to the absolute minimum, if used at all, as too much can produce a rather lush plant with excessive foliage and few flowers.

Pruning is very important: if neglected, the

plants soon look untidy and produce poor displays of flower or foliage. For the purpose of pruning the heathers fall into three groups.

a Winter-flowering varieties. These should be lightly trimmed soon after flowering, in spring; also remove old flower heads and generally tidy up. The flat types such as *E. carnea* 'Springwood White' can also have the spreading stems shortened.

b Summer-flowering and foliage varieties. In early spring prune these back by cutting off the old flowers, as this will encourage good new shoots to give a bright display of flowers in the summer. Foliage types should also be lightly pruned to encourage new growth to give the maximum of new colourful growth.

c Tree heathers. Little pruning is required, except to keep the plants in good shape. This again is best done in the spring and usually involves the tidying up of badly-shaped branches and shoots. If tree heathers do get really out of shape they can occasionally be pruned really hard, as this will encourage plenty of new growth and a better-shaped bush.

Mulching is an important operation carried out ideally every year. The best material is moss peat, but well chopped-up dry bracken will also do well. Autumn is a good time to apply this mulch, but early spring will do equally well.

One great asset of the heathers is their ability to form great mats of ground cover. In this day and age, when we are all looking for ways of having an attractive garden while reducing the work, a heather garden is well worth considering.

One important point to consider if you have an area suitable for massed heather planting is to make sure it is weed-free. Once well established, weeds such as the spreading couch can be very difficult to eradicate and can soon ruin a good planting. So take time to pull out all possible weeds, especially the perennial ones.

The ideal way to plan and plant a heather garden is to be bold and plant good groups of one variety. The smaller ones can be placed about 12 in (30 cm) apart, and the spreading types such as *E. carnea* 'Springwood White' up to 15 in (45 cm) apart. By planting in groups you have patches of colour to give interest all the year.

To add variety you can plant a range of suitable shrubs in between – many interesting shrubs mix in exceptionally well with heathers. As a spot plant to add summer and autumn colour, many of the Japanese Maples will blend in very well – especially the lovely 'Dissectum' forms with finely-cut foliage. The low, dome-like *Berberis thunbergii* 'Atropurpurea Nana' with deep red foliage blends in well; in addition some of the really dwarf rhododendrons look excellent, such as *Rhododendron* 'Carmen' with deep scarlet flowers and low-growing habit. The grey-green foliage of *R. impeditum* also blends in well with a display of purple-blue flowers in the spring. Pernettyas, with their succulent autumn berries in shades of white, pink, red and purple, look good planted with heathers, but should be trimmed well to prevent too much tall growth. Perhaps the best shrubs to include with your heathers are some of the excellent dwarf conifers – the low-growing compact junipers with grey/blue foliage such as *Juniperus squamata* 'Blue Star', the brilliant gold of *Thuja orientalis* 'Aurea Nana', and the neat green cone of *Picea glauca albertiana* 'Conica'. These are just a few ideas among the endless possibilities, to add interest and shape.

Heathers propagate with comparative ease. Depending on the quantity you require, this can be carried out in two ways.

a Layering. Prepare a mix of 50/50 moss peat and limefree sand, spread to a fair depth 1 – 2 in (2.5 – 5 cm) of this mixture around and in the planting. With the more upright-growing forms, cut a few small pegs from the wood or hedgerow and peg into this peat-sand mix a few healthy branches. If you do this in the late summer to early autumn, you should have well-rooted layers for the next summer/autumn, which can then be cut from the parent plant and bedded out in the garden or a nursery bed. With certain of the flat-growing heathers, pegging is really unnecessary. Work plenty of this peat-sand mix in and around the branches to a thickness of 1 – 2 in (2.5 – 5 cm), and these stems will also root in 9 – 12 months.

b Cuttings. During late summer cut off healthy non-flowering shoots about 1 – 1½ in (2.5 – 4 cm) long. With finger and thumb, strip off carefully the bottom ¼ in (6 mm) of leaves. Dip the cuttings into a medium strength of rooting hormone if desired (this is not in fact essential, as the plants will root without this help). The best rooting medium consists of 50/50 moss peat and lime-free sharp sand. Fill a pot or well-drained seed tray with this mixture, firm very lightly to keep the mixture open with plenty of air, insert the cuttings and water in gently.

When the cuttings are settled, sprinkle a light layer of sharp sand on the surface; apart from looking neat this helps to retain some moisture. Keep the cuttings in a cool glasshouse or frame, make sure that they never dry out, and with proper care you should have a high percentage of success, allowing you to transplant the cuttings into a nursery bed the following spring.

With more and more heather varieties being produced, their susceptibility to disease has unfortunately increased. The fungus phytophora cinnamomi has become quite a problem. The first signs of trouble can be seen when the foliage changes from bright green to a rather dull olive green, and the tips gradually die back, eventually causing the whole plant to turn brown and die. Unfortunately, it is difficult if not impossible to control in a small garden; if any signs appear, dig up and burn any affected plants immediately and do not replant heathers in the same soil for a number of years.

When you buy heathers, always make sure that the plants look healthy, and if you grow your own keep all the materials, pots and trays very clean.

Winter-flowering Ericas
Described below are a few of the winter or snow heathers found growing wild in many countries of Southern Europe. This group has the great advantage of tolerating lime in the soil.

E. carnea 'Alan Coates'
This is a compact slightly spreading form with bright green foliage, flowering late winter to early spring with rosy purple flowers.

E. carnea 'December Red'
This vigorous plant has dark green foliage. The bright rose-red flowers show in mid-winter.

E. carnea 'King George'
This old favourite, with compact slightly upright growth, has deep pink flowers which appear first in the depths of winter and continue to give colour even when snow or frost is on the ground.

E. carnea 'Pink Spangles'
With bright green foliage and bright pink flowers, this is a vigorous, spreading plant that will start to flower in mid-winter and continue well into the spring.

E. carnea 'Springwood Pink'
This, a vigorous spreading plant, has flowers that appear initally white, and then change to clear pink. It flowers from late winter until the early spring, and also provides excellent ground cover.

E. carnea 'Springwood White'
This is very similar to E. c. 'Springwood Pink' except that the flowers remain white. It is very free-flowering, and again provides excellent ground cover.

E. carnea 'Vivellii'
The stiff, dark green foliage turns to bronze in the winter.

Erica × darleyensis 'Furzey'

E. × darleyensis 'Darley Dale'

This heather first appeared about 100 years ago at Darley Dale in Yorkshire, England. It is definitely one of the most attractive and reliable of all winter-flowering heathers, with the added advantage again of tolerating lime in the soil. From early winter to early spring, this vigorous plant is a mass of pink flowers. Eventually the plants will grow up to 2 ft (60 cm) in height.

E. × darleyensis 'George Rendall'

This could be described as a compact form of *E. × d.* 'Darley Dale'. It is an attractive and reliable plant producing attractive pink spikes of flower throughout the winter.

E. × darleyensis 'Silberschmelze' (Silver Beads)

This is a white-flowered sport with glossy dark green foliage. The clear white flowers have pronounced brown anthers. Again it is a reliable and free-flowering winter heather.

Summer-flowering Ericas

E. cineria

In the summer months many areas of heathland develop a deep purple haze with the massed flowers of *Erica cineria* or bell heathers. There are now many different cultivars that will produce colour throughout the summer. To grow this heather successfully choose a well-drained sunny site and incorporate plenty of peat at planting time.

83

E. cineria 'Atrosanguinea'

This heather has interesting dark blue-green foliage with bright green new shoots in the spring, and single deep purple flowers in early summer.

E. cineria 'C.D. Eason'

One of the very best summer-flowering heathers, this plant becomes a neat mound of deep green foliage and from early summer is covered in a mass of deep pink flowers.

E. cineria 'Eden Valley'

This cultivar introduces an interesting colour break, producing white flowers with a deep purple flush. It is a compact spreading plant with light green foliage.

E. cineria 'Fiddlers Gold'

This summer-flowering heather has light green foliage, beautifully tipped with yellow and red. The single purple flowers arrive in early summer.

E. cineria 'Tilford'

This very compact and bushy bell heather has bright purple spikes of flower which give interest throughout the summer.

E. vagans 'Lyonesse'

This is one of the best summer-flowering white ericas with attractive brown anthers.

E. vagans 'Mrs. D.F. Maxwell'

This really old favourite has upright foliage which is dark green with light tips. The very deep pink flowers appear in mid-summer. Trim lightly in the spring to remove any dead flowers.

See also *Calluna*.

Escallonia

Here we have a shrub which is evergreen, quick-growing, free-flowering, tolerant of most soils and able to withstand sea conditions bringing salt-laden winds.

In milder climates there is no problem about hardiness, but in colder areas a rather more sheltered position will be necessary. It is excellent if planted as a free-growing shrub, allowing plenty of space for development. It can also form a thick evergreen hedge around 6 – 8 ft (1.8 – 2.4 m) high which flowers freely in the spring. Fairly hard pruning after flowering is essential to encourage young growth and plenty of flower. Escallonias are easy to root from semi-ripe cuttings.

E. 'Apple Blossom'

In this beautiful shrub, the profusion of pale pink flowers contrasts so well with the glossy dark green leaves. It is quite a compact grower, attaining eventually about 5 ft (1.5 m) in height. 'Apple Blossom' also makes a beautiful evergreen hedge covered with a profusion of colour in early summer.

E. 'Crimson Spire'

This is very quick-growing with a distinctive upright habit and bright crimson flowers.

E. 'Donard Radiance'

This hybrid was raised in Northern Ireland at the Sleive Donard Nurseries, which introduced a number of excellent *Escallonia*. It has distinctive deep pink flowers and a definite 'eye' in the middle. This is a vigorous and lovely shrub.

E. macrantha

For seaside planting this is a winner, apparently happy to put up with the most extreme conditions. The bright green glossy leaves are larger than most *Escallonia*, and these offset the large deep pink spring flowers. In ideal conditions this is a very vigorous shrub sending up plenty of new shoots each year. Unfortunately it is also the least hardy *Escallonia* and will only thrive in milder areas, As a hedge it is very good indeed, forming a thick wall of evergreen up to 8 ft (2.4 m) high.

Eucryphia

This is a shrub or small tree that will invariably attract attention. An established bush produces a mass of lovely single white flowers in late summer and it is certainly a surprise to see such a beautiful shrub flowering late in the season. It prefers light shade or a slightly sheltered position. Unfortunately you may have to wait a year or two for the plant to flower freely, but it is certainly worth waiting for. Propagation is by means of summer cuttings.

E. glutinosa

With glossy dark green leaves and abundant flowers in late summer, this deciduous member of the family gives a bonus of autumn colour.

E. × intermedia 'Rostrevor'

This is an open evergreen shrub with small shiny leaves and a mass of white flowers late in the summer. This *Eucryphia* flowers at a young age and is excellent for a small garden.

E. × nymansensis 'Nymansay'

Imagine enormous white flowers up to 2½ in (6 cm) across with a pronounced central bunch of fine stamens! Forming quite an upright bush or small tree up to 15 ft (4.5 m) high, this evergreen in full flower is really lovely.

Euonymus

The deciduous varieties which flourish in chalk are grown for their brilliant autumn colour and unique fruit capsules, which are rose pink outside, showing brilliant orange seeds when they open. The evergreen varieties have several different uses from ground cover to background planting. All the evergreens root easily from semi-ripe cuttings; the deciduous forms can be grown from seed.

Eucryphia × nymansensis 'Nymansay'

E. europaeus 'Red Cascade'

This is the best of the deciduous forms, with brilliant scarlet leaves in the autumn and often laden with lovely pink fruit capsules. It grows eventually to about 6 ft (1.8 m).

E. fortunei 'Emerald and Gold'

A low-growing bushy *Euonymus* forming excellent ground cover, this is native to the USA. It has bright gold and dark green variegated leaves, which in winter are tinged with bronzy pink. Light pruning in the spring encourages the best bright new foliage.

E. fortunei 'Emerald Gaiety'

This is another small-leaved evergreen *Euonymus*

from the USA, but this time the green leaves are margined with white giving an overall silver effect. It is excellent low ground cover and useful for small flower arrangements.

E. japonicus 'Aureo-pictus'

Here is a rather smart upright evergreen with remarkably shiny green leaves with a clear gold mark in the middle, surrounded by a rich shiny green edge. Sometimes this variety is used as a pot plant. Unfortunately not too hardy, it is nevertheless very easy to propagate from cuttings during late summer and autumn.

Exochorda

A very beautiful shrub, *E. × macrantha* 'The Bride' is definitely the best of this genus. Free-flowering, forming a dense mound which is covered in large snow white flowers in late spring, *Exochorda* are not too fussy about soil and will tolerate acid or alkaline types. New shrubs can be easily propagated from summer cuttings.

Fatsia

The striking evergreen *F. japonica* is really exotic-looking. Given a sheltered position in light shade it will grow into a bold spreading evergreen up to 15 ft (4.5 m) high. The flowers are also rather unusual, being panicles of milk-white globular flower heads which appear in autumn. Despite the very large evergreen leaves this shrub thrives in town gardens and will also do well by the sea. There is a variegated form with large white blotches near the end of each leaf. Propagate from summer cuttings.

Forsythia

Spring would not be quite the same without forsythia. It is most exciting when cut early in spring and forced for indoor decoration; those clear single yellow flowers are really lovely when undamaged by wind and rain, and the flower buds are undamaged by the birds! Forsythias are happy on nearly all soils including lime; as quick-growing

shrubs they certainly thrive in fairly rich conditions. Be sure to prune each year after flowering and remove old wood to encourage new growth. If you have a really old plant it is sometimes best to forgo flowers for one year and cut it to the ground. Forsythia also makes an excellent flowering hedge. If you want a really easy shrub to propagate do try this one. Semi-ripe cuttings will root easily during the summer, and failing this, hardwood cuttings pushed into the soil during the autumn will root by the spring.

F. 'Beatrix Farrand'

Developed in the USA, this is a shrub with an erect dense habit, growing to a height of around 8 ft (2.4 m). The very large flowers are soft canary yellow.

F. 'Lynwood'

This is definitely one of the best forsythias, covered each spring in a mass of rich golden flowers.

Fothergilla

F. major is definitely a lime-hater, and perhaps for much of the year it is not the most exciting shrub, with a crop of fluffy white flowers appearing in the spring. It is in the autumn, however, that the *Fothergilla* really come into their own, with a rich display of glorious colour in shades of red, orange and yellow. It must be one of the most beautiful of all autumn shrubs. Plant in an open sunny position to achieve the best from this slow-growing plant. It will root from cuttings but is not easy.

Fremontodendron

F. 'California Glory' is an amazing shrub that has suddenly become very popular. Being a native of California it is not too hardy. Perhaps best suited to growing on a south wall, it appears to thrive on dry, rather poor soil. The enormous, rich yellow almost wax-like flowers appear in late spring and carry on through to mid-summer; by the end of

Fremontodendron 'California Glory'

the summer the shrub can look quite exhausted from producing such an abundance of flowers. It can be quite a vigorous plant and may need some pruning. The stems and leaves are covered in a curious gritty dust rather like itching powder. Propagation is not easy; soft cuttings taken during the summer will root in an open compost. *F.* 'California Glory' is excellent in a cool conservatory, either in a tub or planted on a wall – but beware, because it can get fairly large.

Fuchsia

This is certainly one of the most popular of all flowering shrubs. The majority sold during late spring and summer are too tender to withstand the average winter, but fortunately there is a selection of hardy varieties which are excellent garden plants. There are some excellent hybrids which combine hardiness with a long flowering period. There are compact growing varieties and others reaching 4 – 5 ft (1.2 – 1.5 m) in height.

Perhaps another reason why fuchsias are so popular is because they are easy to propagate from semi-ripe cuttings in the summer. Tolerant of sun or shade and happy in most well-drained soils, the hardy fuchsias are excellent garden shrubs. In most areas plants will die back each winter and should be pruned to ground level in the spring.

F. 'Alice Hoffman'

This form has attractive dark green foliage with a purple tinge; the small flowers are scarlet outside with white petals.

F. magellanica 'Variegata'

Here we have the added bonus of attractive

87

foliage, as the leaves have a light edge and are tinged with pink. The flowers are small, scarlet and purple. This is an easy-going and vigorous fuchsia which can brighten a dark corner.

F. 'Mrs. Popple'

This is one of the most vigorous of the hardy fuchsias, eventually growing up to 4 ft (1.2 m) and equally bushy. The large flowers are scarlet and violet.

F. 'Tom Thumb'

This really charming shrub has an excellent compact habit and grows to a maximum of 12 – 15 in (30 – 38 cm) in height. It is extremely free-flowering, producing a mass of scarlet and violet flowers.

Garrya

Any shrub that brightens up the dull winter days is worth a place in the garden. When growing in ideal conditions *G. elliptica* is a really outstanding plant. It is a native of California, evergreen with dark leathery leaves; not too hardy in colder areas where a sheltered wall is required. In common with a number of shrubs there is a male and female form. It is essential that you plant the male form which produces a mass of magnificent grey-green catkins in winter when really the garden is fairly dull. Perhaps it is seen at its best growing on a wall where it can be kept in trim. *Garrya* can also make a magnificent hedge which combines a useful evergreen with winter colour. It is tempting to cut large sprays of catkins for indoor decoration but, unfortunately, it does spread a mass of golden pollen. *Garrya* thrive in fairly poor dry soil and are happy in an open sunny position.

This is a fairly difficult shrub to propagate but ripe cuttings taken in autumn will usually root with a little bottom heat. Above all they strongly resent any root disturbance, and to overcome this it is best to put the cuttings in a small peat pot filled with sharp sand; they can then be potted on without any check.

G. elliptica 'James Roof' is an extra vigorous

Garrya elliptica

male form, with remarkable catkins up to 12 in (30 cm) long.

Gaultheria

The acid-soil-loving *Gaultheria* species are not the most popular of shrubs, but if you have space and suitable semi-woodland conditions *G. shallon* is worth growing for the lovely sprays of pink tinged lily-of-the-valley-like flowers, followed by deep purple fruits. It is an evergreen with tough, leathery leaves. Under ideal growing conditions it can become a menace, spreading by means of underground runners. Propagation is best carried out by seed sowed from the ripe fruits. It can also be grown from runners and will root (but not too easily) from cuttings.

Gaultheria shallon

Genista

In this genus, there are one or two very useful shrubs which are happy in acid or alkaline soils and will tolerate hot dry sun conditions. Closely allied to the brooms, all *Genista* species have yellow pea-like flowers and are generally very free-flowering.

Regular pruning is essential and this should be done immediately after flowering. If left unpruned a rather untidy bush will develop from any member of this genus. Propagation is quite easy from cuttings taken in the summer.

G. aetnensis (Mount Etna Broom)

Almost a small tree, this lovely shrub is found growing wild on the slopes of Mount Etna, Sicily. Out of flower it assumes the appearance of a light feathery tree with drooping, rush-like stems. In summer it is covered in a mass of bright yellow pea-like flowers. This species can grow up to 20 ft (6 m) in height, therefore it needs placing carefully. A little light pruning will help to keep a

dense bushy plant. Probably the best method of propagation is from seed.

G. hispanica (Spanish Gorse)

This is a low-growing and very prickly shrub with fine foliage. One great asset of this genus is that the plants tolerate very dry conditions, so *G. hispanica* is well suited to planting on a dry, well-drained bank. In fact it makes excellent ground cover, achieving a final height of 18 in (45 cm). The whole bush is covered in a mass of yellow flowers in early summer. A light trim after flowering is essential to keep the bush compact. Propagation from summer cuttings is quite easy.

G. lydia

This is a low-growing, compact plant which absolutely smothers itself in bright yellow flowers during early summer. With a slightly drooping habit it can be used to excellent effect to hang over a wall, but is equally effective at the front of a shrub border. Final height is around 2 ft (60 cm) and about the same width. To keep a good shape and ensure plenty of flower it is essential to carry out an annual prune soon after flowering. Summer cuttings in pure sand root fairly easily.

Griselinia

A unique feature of the fast-growing evergreen *G. littoralis* is the fresh light green of the foliage. Sadly not too hardy, it is an excellent hedging plant in milder areas. It is also extremely tolerant of seaside conditions. Under ideal conditions, this native of New Zealand makes rapid growth and needs to be pruned each summer.

As an alternative to a hedge it can be left to grow into a round bush growing up to 10 – 15 ft (3 – 4.5 m) in height, which will form an excellent evergreen screen. There is also a variegated form called 'Dixon's Cream' which is useful in flower arrangements. *Griselinia* is easy to propagate from summer cuttings.

Genista lydia

X Halimiocistus

Here are one or two useful shrubs which flower for a long period and are well suited to the front of a shrub border or spreading over paving. The main flowering time is summer, but this can often be extended into early autumn. To achieve the best results, plant in a hot dry sunny position and give a light trim after flowering. All will root from summer cuttings.

X H. ingwersenii

This species forms a dense round bush about 18 in (45 cm) high. It produces a mass of simple white flowers each with a centre bunch of yellow stamens.

X H. wintonensis

This is a rather weak plant, but it is certainly worth a try because the flowers have some of the most beautiful markings. The foliage is light grey. Simple, pure white flowers have smart yellow and maroon markings in the base, giving a very alert effect. Well-drained soil and hot sunny conditions are essential requirements.

Halimium

H. lasianthum, a low-growing evergreen shrub, comes from the hills of southern Portugal. As might be expected, an open sunny position is essential, with good drainage. The grey foliage acts as an excellent foil to the beautiful, clear yellow flowers with their dark maroon blotch in the base giving a very striking effect. Root from summer cuttings.

Hamamelis (Witch Hazel)

Perhaps king of all winter-flowering shrubs, nothing cheers up a dull winter garden quite like the witch hazels. Apparently, early settlers in North America used twigs of the native *H. virginiana* for water divining. Because of this, it was supposed that the shrub had magical properties, hence the name witch hazel.

To achieve the best display of winter flowers, try to choose an open site with plenty of leafmould or peat worked into the soil. Certainly this is not a fast-growing genus but after many years large specimens can be seen 20 – 30 ft (6 – 9 m) high, so allow plenty of space. Pruning is normally quite unnecessary. If the occasional branch tends to upset the shape of your bush then it can be safely trimmed back in the summer.

This is an expensive shrub, mainly because it is slow-growing and very difficult to propagate. Nearly all the plants sold at present are grafted onto seedlings of *H. virginiana*. The seed takes up to two years to germinate, then a further year to produce a small graft, so a lot of work goes into producing this lovely plant. Its position in the garden is important; if you can arrange a dark green background it will show off the yellow flowers effectively. If you are lucky enough to be in a mild, rhododendron-growing area, try an association with the early-flowering *Rhododendron* 'Tessa' or the lavender-flowered *R.* 'Praecox'.

H. × intermedia 'Diane'

This variety comes closest to having bright red flowers; in fact they are coppery orange. It is quite an exciting colour, but placing the shrub against a good background is essential to achieve the best effect. Rich autumn leaf colour gives an added bonus.

H. × intermedia 'Jelena' ('Copper Beauty')

A fairly vigorous *Hamamelis* with large clusters of coppery-red flowers, *H.* × *i.* 'Jelena' also puts on an excellent display of orange and flame autumn colour.

H. mollis (Chinese Witch Hazel)

This is the most widely planted of all *Hamamelis*. From early winter to early spring the bare branches are covered in a mass of rich golden flowers, with a deep purple stain at the base of each petal. Each flower consists of a bunch of feathery petals, and apart from brightening the dull winter scene, these have the added bonus of a sweet scent, giving the first hint of spring. The leaves are covered in fine silver hairs which give a grey sheen. Compared with other *Hamamelis*, this one does not particularly shine when it comes to autumn colour.

H. mollis 'Pallida'

The flowers are larger than those of *H. mollis* and bright primrose yellow in colour. The lighter colour definitely highlights this lovely winter-flowering shrub. The gold and orange-flowered forms are also lovely, but their flowers can be lost against a poor background.

Hebe

This is a very large family of shrubs native to New Zealand. Unfortunately many of them are not too hardy. At one time many were included under the name *Veronica*, but this has now been changed and the majority are listed under *Hebe*.

Quick-growing and free-flowering over many months, they are very effective shrubs. Nearly all *Hebe* are easy to propagate from summer cuttings, so keep a few small plants in a sheltered spot as replacements after a cold winter. Plant always in full sun, and they usually benefit from a light prune after flowering.

Hamamelis mollis 'Pallida'

H. albicans

This is quite a striking plant making a dense, dome-shaped bush about 2 ft (60 cm) high. The leaves are a distinctive light grey colour with white flowers appearing late in the spring. It is a useful neat shrub for a sheltered site.

H. × andersonii

Lovely racemes of soft mauve flowers are produced by this species during late summer to early autumn. There is also a striking variegated form. This is a quick-growing shrub but sadly it is not very hardy.

H. 'Autumn Glory'

This is quite a hardy variety which grows up to about 2½ ft (75 cm) in height. It features shiny green leaves with a hint of bronze to purple. Violet blue flowers start in early summer and carry on well into the autumn.

H. brachysiphon

This makes an excellent evergreen but must be trimmed early in the year to keep a good shape. A mass of tiny green leaves cover this dome-like shrub, followed by short spiky white flowers during summer. As one of the hardier members of this genus it can be useful to make a low hedge.

Hebe salicifolia

H. 'Carl Teschner'

This can be very effectively used as ground cover, rarely growing taller than 8 – 10 in (20 – 25 cm) and spreading 3 – 4 ft (90 – 120 cm) over the ground. In summer the whole shrub is covered in a mass of intense violet flowers.

H. × franciscana 'Blue Gem'

This is a very popular hybrid that grows to around 4 ft (1.2 m) in height, forming a neat round bush with racemes of bright blue flowers during the summer. It is fairly hardy. There is also an attractive form with variegated leaf margins.

H. 'Great Orme'

An excellent summer shrub, this *Hebe* gives colour over many months. Making a fairly open bush, the 2 – 3 in (5 – 7.5 cm) long spikes of flower open a deep pink and fade to white at the base. It is fairly hardy.

H. hulkeana

Sadly this species is not too hardy and certainly requires a warm sheltered site. It is quite a low-growing untidy shrub, eventually reaching 3 – 4 ft (90 – 120 cm) in height. The leaves are quite remarkably glossy, and beautiful racemes of loose lavender blue flowers appear during the summer.

H. 'Midsummer Beauty'

This is certainly a very popular *Hebe* with bright green leaves and long racemes of lavender flowers throughout the summer. It needs a fairly sheltered site.

H. salicifolia

The flowers are an interesting combination of white with a soft lilac tint. This is a quick-growing, fairly open shrub up to 5 or 6 ft (1.5 – 1.8 m) high. If damaged in a cold winter, cut the shrub back hard in the spring and often it will sprout away again from the base. This applies to many of the *Hebe* varieties.

Hibiscus

Rather a surprising shrub is the *Hibiscus*, suddenly producing a mass of flower in early autumn when so much is finished. The shrub itself is surprisingly hardy; it will thrive in a sunny, well-drained position. Given a fine start to the autumn these shrubs add a wonderful splash of late colour to the garden. In the less favoured areas some shelter may be required to protect such late flowers from rain and wind. Any pruning should be carried out during the spring, because all *Hibiscus* flower on the current year's growth. Generally they are fairly neat-growing and require little attention.

Propagation is from semi-ripe cuttings, which root fairly easily but sometimes die out during the first winter. Watch out for slugs, which are very partial to the young plants.

H. syriacus 'Blue Bird'

This form bears striking, single violet/blue flowers with the distinctive dark red eye in the base, plus a large central group of pronounced yellow stamens so typical of all Hibiscus.

H. syriacus 'Diana'

The large, pure white single flowers on *H. s.* 'Diana' are really lovely.

H. syriacus 'Woodbridge'

This has rose-pink flowers with a deeper red stain at the base; it is certainly a beautiful *Hibiscus*.

Hippophae (Sea Buckthorn)

H. rhamnoides is perhaps rather a neglected shrub, so often only considered for seaside planting. It is a hardy, prickly shrub that once established will withstand all extremes of wind and salt air, eventually forming a dense thicket. One slight drawback for garden use is that the shrub is unisexual, similar to holly. Only the female plants will produce berries and at least one male plant is required to pollinate five or six females. Insist when buying Sea Buckthorn that you have the correct mix of male to female plants. Apart from seaside use it will thrive inland and make a very attractive deciduous shrub, covered much of the year in silvery willow-like leaves. The female plants produce a mass of attractive light orange berries which are filled with intensely acid juice, and even in the depths of winter the birds will leave them alone.

Seed is probably the best way to produce more plants but of course it is not easy to distinguish between a batch of male and female seedlings. In winter it *is* possible to distinguish, because the buds on male plants are conical and conspicuous, whereas on the female they are smaller and rounded.

Hydrangea

This is a large and very varied group of shrubs which plays an important role in the garden. Apart from being fairly easy-going they do add colour during summer when there is not too much about. Added to this the flower heads turn lovely

shades of green, purple and red in the autumn, giving excellent material for the flower arrangers.

To achieve the best results there are one or two basic rules. Do not plant in frost pockets; the shrubs generally are quite hardy but new growth appears very early each spring on the bare stem and this is very susceptible to spring frost and keen winds. Plenty of moisture in the soil is important. Incorporate plenty of peat or well-rotted manure when you plant. Also a good mulch each year of leaf-mould, peat, bark or bracken will certainly help to conserve moisture. The hot dry summer of 1983 certainly made many hydrangeas look very sad indeed and no doubt there was plenty of dead wood to prune out in spring 1984. The large 'mophead' varieties are probably seen at their best in full sun and they really thrive in seaside gardens where they put up a fantastic display. The flat-flowered lacecaps are usually seen at their best in light shade.

How and when to prune is one of the most common questions. Although hydrangeas in winter appear as a bunch of thin twigs which look as if they ought to be pruned, generally prune as little as possible and confine most of this to the spring. Firstly remove any old and dead wood, prune back to a pair of buds any tips with dieback, otherwise apart from any necessary shaping leave the plant alone. Light pruning can be done in the summer, taking certain stems back to a double bud which may develop flower buds the following year.

A further problem with hydrangeas is the riddle of why some gardens get lovely deep blue flowers yet the same variety in another garden turns a rather mauve colour. The answer here is that hydrangeas prefer a rich acid soil when they will give really blue flowers. On alkaline soils the same shrub will need a fortnightly dressing of blueing powder (aluminium sulphate). Also on soils high in lime considerable yellowing Chlorosis can appear on the leaves; to rectify this give a foliar feed of sequestrene or a dressing of iron sulphate at the rate of ¼ oz (7 g) per square yard (m²) watered in with a gallon (4.5 litres) of water.

Hibiscus syriacus 'Blue Bird'

You may begin to think that this is rather a fussy plant, but really under most conditions hydrangeas grow for many years giving little trouble. One thing about them that is really easy is propagation, and cuttings of semi-ripe new growth will root quickly in summer. It is probably wise to root them directly into a small pot as they are so vigorous.

The most widely planted are forms of *Hydrangea macrophylla*, and here we have a division between the round mopheads and the more delicate lacecaps.

Hortensia types

Among the mophead or hortensia types some of the best are the following.

H. macrophylla 'Ami Pasquier' – deep red.
H. macrophylla 'Europa' – large deep pink flowers.
H. macrophylla 'King George' – rose pink.
H. macrophylla 'Emile Moulliere' – lovely round white heads with a blue centre.

Lacecap types

The best of the lacecap varieties, with their flat corymbs of flower, are the following.

H. macrophylla 'Blue Wave'

This is a lovely shrub and one of the most popular lacecap hydrangeas. It is a very strong-growing plant, achieving 6 ft (1.8 m) in height and almost as much in width, so make sure that you allow plenty of space. On acid soils the flowers are rich blue but can vary on more alkaline soils to a mixture of blue and pink or pure pink. It also has very bold dark green foliage.

H. macrophylla 'Lanarth White'

This is a fairly compact variety growing to about 3 ft (90 cm) in height, and it is quite happy in an open sunny position. Pure white florets surround a central bunch of blue fertile flowers, making a lovely combination of colours. Both acid and alkaline soil are suitable; at least the white hydrangeas do not change colour!

H. macrophylla 'Veitchii'

This is quite a tall-growing plant, up to 6 ft (1.8 m) and rather untidy in habit. The flowers are extra large white with a centre of fertile blue flowers. The flowers fade to pink and sometimes green in the shade. If well supported by other shrubs, the untidy habit can be disguised.

H. macrophylla 'White Wave'

This variety is more vigorous than *H. m.* 'Lanarth White' growing to around 5 ft (1.5 m) in height with very free-flowering flat flowers. These comprise a central base of blue fertile flowers surrounded by pure white ray flowers.

H. serrata 'Bluebird'

Moving to a slightly different branch of the genus, this is a lovely delicate hydrangea with a mass of small blue flowers.

H. serrata 'Preziosa'

This is a distinctive variety with small mophead type flowers which start off pink and gradually change to deep crimson. The foliage and stems have a purple tinge.

H. serrata 'Rosalba'

Rather upright in habit, this hydrangea grows to about 4 ft (1.2 m). The flowers start off a very soft pink in colour, gradually fading to white with prominent deep red blotches. This is definitely a good hydrangea for a small garden.

H. paniculata 'Tardiva'

This variety gives a late display of white flowers in autumn.

Hydrangea macrophylla 'Veitchii'

H. villosa

This hydrangea is rather rangy in habit with light brown peeling stems and hairy, somewhat fleshy, leaves. The typical flat flowers include a lovely combination of blue and pink. It is only worth trying, sadly, in milder climates, as very cold weather can be disastrous.

H. paniculata 'Grandiflora'

Here, in contrast, we have an excellent shrub totally different to both lacecaps and mopheads. It is an upright growing deciduous shrub reaching 8 ft (2.4 m) in height.

To achieve the best results plant in a rich loamy soil and mulch regularly with rotted manure or compost. You will be rewarded by large white plumes of flower in mid-summer, which slowly become tinged with pink as the flowers age. Prune back lightly in the spring before growth begins.

Hydrangea paniculata 'Grandiflora'

Hypericum

This is one genus that should cause few problems. All *Hypericum* have the same distinctive open yellow flowers; in some of the dwarf rockery types the flower is smaller but still very distinctive. They are not too fussy about soil and are capable of thriving in the sun or shade; they have a long flowering period, mid-summer to mid-autumn, some interesting foliage and attractive berries. Added to all these advantages, *Hypericum* are quick-growing and very easy to propagate. Semi-ripe cuttings taken from new growth during the summer will easily root.

H. calycinum

Commonly known as Rose of Sharon or St John's

Wort, this is one of the most useful and popular ground cover shrubs, especially if you need to cover a fairly large area. As a shrub that only grows around 12 in (30 cm) high it bears surprisingly large flowers in mid-summer. The flowers form large yellow globes with a mass of fine stamens in the centre. To keep the plants in good condition go over with shears each spring and you will keep getting fresh new growth each year. If left, this variety can look rather untidy. This is a fairly invasive plant that spreads via underground suckers. It will root from cuttings quite easily; seed is another method of propagation; or simply dig up and plant the runners.

H. 'Hidcote'

One of the most popular of all garden shrubs, and almost evergreen in character, it forms a fairly large bush up to 6 ft (1.8 m) in height and equally thick. It is happy in most soils, sun or shade, and flowers almost continuously from mid-summer to mid-autumn. Prune hard each spring if you want a vigorous bush and plenty of deep yellow flowers.

H. × inodorum 'Elstead'

In flower this is definitely not one of the most exciting forms of *Hypericum*; the most attractive feature is the lovely sealing wax red berries that appear in summer. Towards the end of summer some berries turn black, others are still red and the bush is also flowering, giving a lovely overall effect. It produces a large number of seedlings each year, which can become a problem.

H. patulum 'Sungold'

Keep up the spring pruning and you will get a display of attractive olive to yellow foliage from this form. Well placed in light shade, these golden foliage *Hypericum* can be very effective. The flower performance is not so good, however, and yellow flowers with yellow foliage are not the best combination.

H. × moseranum 'Tricolor'

Definitely the most striking foliage of all *Hypericum* varieties can be found on this delicate plant, the leaves combining the colours of olive green, cream and deep pink. Added to the foliage, you get the bonus of large clear yellow flowers. Not so tall, growing around 3 ft (90 cm). Unfortunately, cold winters can damage this shrub but usually new growth will spring up again from the base.

H. 'Rowallane'

This variety is native to Northern Ireland and is perhaps the most delicate of all in habit and sadly not too hardy. The charm of this lovely shrub is the weeping habit and the shape of the rich deep yellow flowers. Unlike many *Hypericum* varieties that open their flowers boldly to the sun, on *H.* 'Rowallane' they hang in a rather shy fashion.

Ilex (Holly)

In Great Britain, Christmas would not be quite the same without a few sprigs of berried holly. Often it is a race with the birds to get there first. Apart from the common holly of hedgerows and woods there are many others that are very useful garden evergreens. As well as interesting variegated foliage, the bright red and sometimes yellow berries brighten the winter scene. One snag with the hollies is that they are dioecious, which in simple terms means that the female flowers are on one bush and the male flowers on the other. Only female plants will produce berries and this is why some wild hollies produce frequent crops of berries and others never do. There are one or two exceptions which are self-fertilising and will berry on their own.

Hollies are not fast-growing shrubs but eventually make excellent thick evergreens. A really good holly hedge takes a lot of beating, and even under the most polluted urban environment hollies will grow.

Propagation from late summer cuttings is not too difficult; usually a little bottom heat will encourage a better rooting percentage.

I. × altaclarensis 'Golden King'

Almost smooth leaves distinguish this bold variegated holly. The leaves have a central splash of green surrounded by gold, and it is a female holly which will produce a crop of berries.

I. × altaclarensis 'Lawsoniana'

This bears some of the most attractive of all variegated holly leaves, combining yellow, olive and green with virtually no prickles. They are fairly large leaves similar in appearance to *Elaeagnus* 'Maculata Aurea'. Certainly a good holly for the flower arranger, this is another female plant.

I. aquifolium

This is the common holly, which can grow into a fairly massive tree up to 80 ft (24 m) high. It is perhaps most useful as a hedging plant or

Ilex × altaclarensis 'Lawsoniana'

background screen. Holly has one big advantage over many evergreens – it remains dense with foliage to the ground. If you find a good berrying form try rooting this from summer cuttings.

I. aquifolium 'Argenteo-marginata'

This is a popular and useful variegated holly with a white edge to the prickly leaves. The majority are female and can look very attractive covered in a crop of red berries.

I. aquifolium 'Ferox Argentea' (Hedgehog Holly)

This one is quite a curiosity, as it has prickly spines all round the edge of each leaf, as well as clusters all over the leaf surface, producing a strange

Kalmia latifolia 'Clementine Churchill'

effect. Apart from the silver variegated form there is another with gold variegation.

I. aquifolium 'Golden Milkboy'

The shiny leaves of this variety have perhaps the most bold green and gold markings of any holly I know. Unfortunately it has one fault; odd shoots keep reverting back to plain green and must always be cut out, otherwise you will end up with a green holly. There is also a form called 'Silver Milkboy' or 'Cornish Cream', which is not quite as striking as the gold. Sadly both are male hollies, so there are no berries.

I. aquifolium 'Handsworth New Silver'

Of all the silver hollies this is probably the very best. The stems have a distinctive purple tinge and bear rather larger than usual leaves with silver and green variegations. It is also female, giving the possibility of berries.

I. aquifolium 'J.C. van Tol'

Here is a fairly smooth-leaved green holly that defies all the rules and is self-fertilising; therefore just one plant will produce plenty of berries. Perhaps rather more open in habit than the common green holly, it does make an excellent hedge, especially when full of berry. There is also a form called 'Golden van Tol' with variegated leaves.

I. aquifolium 'Pyramidalis Fructuluteo'

This is another form which has yellow berries. If you want a change for the winter try this one.

Kalmia

Commonly called the Calico Bush or Mountain Laurel, *K. latifolia* is a beautiful evergreen that grows wild over wide areas of North America. To achieve success this shrub requires much the same conditions as rhododendrons, that is, cool, moist acid soil, but for preference a sunny position. It eventually forms a dense evergreen shrub with very glossy leaves and about 10 ft (3 m) high. Usually coming into flower just after most rhododendrons have finished, it fills a useful early summer gap. The pink flowers have great charm, forming small clusters of delicate pink cups. There is also an excellent deep red form called *K. l.* 'Clementine Churchill'. The *Kalmia* species have been rather neglected and, as so many plants wax and wane in popularity, so we may hope to see a renewed interest fairly soon.

Propagation of the ordinary forms is best done by seed, but it is very slow. Cuttings will root with special care but they are not at all easy.

Kerria

K. japonica 'Pleniflora', with double flowers, is the most popular of this genus; it is a fairly easy shrub and well worth planting for spring colour.

K. japonica 'Golden Guinea'

This is an exciting new introduction that will surely become popular. The flowers are the same distinctive orange *Kerria* colour but much larger and single. It may well transform the common old *Kerria* into something quite special!

Kolkwitzia

High in the mountains of China the delightful shrub *K. amabilis* 'Pink Cloud' was discovered at the beginning of the century. It is definitely one of the easy shrubs, growing happily under nearly all soil conditions. When you buy a young plant it initially appears rather thin and weak, but fairly quickly a bushy 8 – 10 ft (2.4 – 3 m) shrub will develop, so allow plenty of room. During late spring the whole plant is a mass of soft pink bell-like flowers. Each year prune back soon after flowering, removing any weak shoots and dead wood. Propagation is very easily achieved from summer cuttings.

Laurus (Bay)

The bay tree, *L. nobilis*, is a useful evergreen shrub, and apart from an occasional scorch from the wind it is quite hardy. One asset is that it is happy to be clipped and kept to modest proportions. Large numbers are grown as pyramids or pompoms and planted in tubs. Sadly, many of these fail to survive very long, perhaps due to lack of water during the summer, or to cold winter winds. Bay is an evergreen that thrives by the seaside and can form an excellent thicket or hedge.

It is another shrub which like the holly has male flowers on one bush and female on another. The rather interesting fluffy yellow flowers are followed on the female by shiny black berries. Propagation is from summer cuttings or seed.

Lavandula (Lavender)

There is something very endearing about lavender, which conjures up visions of hot summer days with the bees busily working at the flowers. The superb, rich smell of the foliage adds to the charm of this dwarf shrub.

All lavenders are fairly easy-going with a preference for dry, well-drained soil and of course full sun. This is an excellent shrub to form a low, silver hedge. To keep a good shape it is essential to keep the bushes well pruned; otherwise you soon get an untidy, scruffy-looking bush. Old flower heads can be trimmed off and dried to make a scented pot-pourri of flowers and petals. The main pruning should be carried out in spring when the bushes should be quite severely cut back.

Propagation from summer cuttings is quite easy. You can grow lavender from seed but the resulting plants will be very varied.

L. augustifolia 'Hidcote'

Probably the best of all, this is a fairly dwarf

lavender growing to around 15 in (38 cm). Large, intense blue flowers show up well against the silver foliage in mid-summer.

L. augustifolia 'Munstead'

This is another fairly compact variety, flowering in mid-summer. The large flowers are rather pale in colour. There are in the lavender genus both white and pink flowering forms, as well as the more familiar blue.

Leptospermum

This genus is definitely a gamble, because even in milder areas a very cold winter will kill this shrub off. Despite this it is worth trying. Fortunately it is quick-growing and easy to strike from summer cuttings. They are mainly natives of Australia and New Zealand, so look for a sheltered corner or sunny wall for winter protection, with preferably an acid or neutral soil.

L. scoparium 'Red Damask'

Many of the *Leptospermum* varieties have white flowers, but this lovely shrub has distinctive deep red, small double flowers which absolutely cover the whole bush. The flowers are like flat little roses clinging close to the stem. The feathery foliage is a deep green to bronze in colour. Ultimately growing to around 6 ft (1.8 m) this is a beautiful shrub when the winter allows it to survive.

Leucothoe

L. fontanesiana 'Rainbow' is an evergreen that thrives in moist acid soil. The main attraction of this particular variety is the spectacular variegation on the leaves, combining streaks of purple, pink, yellow and green. The early spring growth can be quite dramatic and it is very useful for flower arrangements. Propagation is fairly easy by means of rooted cuttings.

Lippia

The Lemon-scented Verbena (*L. citriodora*) is not a very hardy plant, but the foliage when picked and crushed gives off the most delicious scent, combining the sharp smell of lemon with verbena. It is a plant of the warm south and should be sited against a warm wall where it will enjoy the hot summer sun. This is a deciduous plant which grows up to 8 ft (2.4 m), with rather insignificant sprays of pale lavender flowers which appear in late summer. It is fairly easy to propagate from cuttings, so keep a spare young plant on hand in case the winter takes its toll.

Lonicera (Honeysuckle)

We have here a very large genus, perhaps best known for the various climbers and twiners which make excellent wall and trellis plants. Of the shrubby kind there are a number of useful plants which on first sight bear very little resemblance to the more popular climbing honeysuckle. All honeysuckles are easy to grow and will tolerate most soil conditions. They will also root easily from cuttings.

L. fragrantissima

This is a rather twiggy shrub which is generally evergreen but can lose many leaves during severe winter weather. Its popularity is due to the very early display of delicate winter flowers. These creamy white, very fragrant flowers start in early winter and can continue into early spring. Certainly a worthwhile shrub to include in a sheltered corner. It will grow up to 6 ft (1.8 m) in height, but is never the most exciting shrub when not in flower.

L. nitida

This is an easy-going evergreen shrub that is mainly used to form a low thick hedge; it is happy in the majority of soil types, the mass of shiny green leaves forming a thick barrier. It can form a very neat box-shaped hedge when clipped, but beware a heavy fall of snow, as this can do great

Magnolia liliiflora 'Nigra'

damage and break the hedge apart. In fact the whole shrub can be cut hard to the ground, and this may sometimes be beneficial when the shrub becomes too woody. It is easy to propagate even from hardwood cuttings stuck into the open ground. To make a good hedge, try to obtain the cultivar *L. t.* 'Yunnan'.

L. nitida 'Baggessen's Gold'

The ordinary green form of *L.nitida* is really rather boring as a free-growing shrub, but this is not true of the gold form which is fairly low-growing, with a mass of small golden leaves. Carefully placed it can be a very effective shrub.

L. pileata

This shrub makes a dense, low-growing evergreen which can make very attractive ground cover.

L. tatarica 'Hack's Red'

Raised in Canada, this is the best form of the species. It is a very vigorous shrub growing up to 8 ft (2.4 m) in height. It is very rough and hardy, putting on a showy display of red flowers in early summer.

Magnolia

Without any doubt we have here some of the most exciting and aristocratic shrubs in the garden. To add a touch of class to your spring display the magnolias are essential. Over the past few years they have ceased to be relatively rare and are now available in a wide range of varieties; in fact some of the exciting new forms are also slowly gaining in popularity.

It is a shrub that requires very careful placing in the garden, and consideration must be given to eventual size and above all shelter. Unfortunately, late spring frost and cold winds so often ruin the vulnerable flowers. Close association with other shrubs or a dense screen behind will all help to give protection during these vulnerable spring weeks.

Magnolias have very fleshy roots which are easily damaged, but as the majority are now grown in containers it is possible to plant with a minimum of disturbance. Prepare a good planting hole at least 2×2 ft (60×60 cm) and work in plenty of peat or well-rotted compost; a mulch of peat around the stem will also be helpful. Magnolias require a neutral to acid soil, but fortunately there are one or two excellent garden varieties that tolerate lime.

Pruning can be safely carried out during late summer or early spring. As these shrubs are relatively slow-growing, it is unlikely that any pruning will be necessary, except to shape the shrub during the first year or so. In later years *M. × soulangiana* and *M. × loebneri* varieties can grow very large and require some attention to keep them within bounds.

An annual mulch of well-rotted manure or peat with a light dressing of nitrogen (preferably sulphate of ammonia) will keep the plants healthy. Do not be too alarmed if the leaves of your magnolia look rather sick and yellow soon after flowering: this is quite characteristic. The leaves become healthy and green in mid-summer. Propagation is not too difficult, and semi-ripe shoots, about $3 - 4$ in ($7.5 - 10$ cm) long, from the current year's growth, will root fairly easily with the aid of some bottom heat.

M. liliiflora

This is a rather untidy shrub, eventually growing to around 12 ft (2.5 m) in height. The large 'Tulip Form' flowers are flushed with purple, and it has the advantage of flowering from spring to early summer which is later than many magnolias. Consequently it can escape the spring frost. It requires an acid soil.

M. liliiflora 'Nigra'

Very compact with deep purple flowers and dark green leaves, this one is again late-flowering – in fact sometimes producing a few flowers all through the summer. It also requires an acid soil.

M. liliiflora × stellata hybrids

Recently bred in America is a new race of magnolia hybrids. They are compact, a habit no doubt obtained from the parent *M. stellata*, and the ultimate height will probably be around $6 - 8$ ft ($2 - 3$ m). They flower late in the spring which avoids much of the frost, and produce a mass of deep purple flowers. Two of the very best that we have seen so far are 'Susan' and 'Jane'. Before long they should prove to be very popular for small or large gardens.

M. × loebneri 'Leonard Messel'

This variety and the one below are both excellent garden shrubs that will grow happily with or without lime. Closely related to *M. × l.* 'Merrill', the main difference here is the flower colour. The rather strap-like flowers are fairly deep pink in bud, turning to soft lilac when fully out.

M. × loebneri 'Merrill'

The main characteristics of this lovely magnolia are a neat upright habit and a profusion of medium size, white goblet flowers in the spring. It is quite quick-growing and will begin to flower at an early stage. Bushes can grow up to 25 ft (10 m) high so allow for growth.

M. × soulangiana

Probably the most widely planted of all magnolias, this species is quite often described as the 'Tulip Tree' due to the enormous, white flushed pink goblets of flower which appear on the bare stems. Flowering in spring the flowers are very susceptible to frost. Take care to allow plenty of space in the garden as all the *M. × soulangiana* types eventually form a large 25 ft (7.5 m) high tree and can spread equally wide. It is a shrub that

Magnolia stellata 'Water Lily'

has a surprising tolerance of urban conditions and is often seen at its best in town gardens. There are a number of very good clones giving a range of colour from white to deep purple.

M. × soulangiana 'Alba Superba'

This has very fragrant white flowers, and forms a fairly erect bush.

M. × soulangiana 'Lennei'

One of the most beautiful, and possibly later in flower than others, this features very large goblet-shaped flowers which are a beautiful shade of rose to purple outside, and white within. The leaves are much larger than most of the *M. × soulangiana* types. If you are lucky, sometimes a second

flush of flowers will appear in the autumn.

M. × soulangiana 'Picture'

A vigorous shrub showing a definite upright habit, this variety has dark green, rather tough leaves and large dark pink flowers.

M. × soulangiana 'Rustica Rubra'

With rich rosy red flowers, this is a fast-growing magnolia.

M. stellata

For the small garden this is a winner! It forms a dense, compact plant which produces a mass of fragrant white flowers which appear ahead of the leaves. It is not very fast-growing but will eventually achieve around 15 ft (4.5 m). Quite often known as the 'Star Magnolia' because of the lovely flower shape, this is a beautiful spring shrub that associates well with dwarf bulbs.

M. stellata 'Rosea'

Flowers of this variety open to a lovely soft pink. Otherwise it is similar in every way to *M. stellata*.

M. stellata 'Water Lily'

Choose this one for larger white flowers with more petals.

M. thompsoniana

This magnolia flowers during the summer and has a very strong scent. It forms a rather wide spreading plant with large pale green leaves which are grey underneath. The large flowers are creamy yellow in colour.

M. wilsonii

Here is a total change in flower shape. This deciduous magnolia could be described as a small tree or certainly a large shrub. The sweet-scented white flowers hang down like large bells, and in

Magnolia × loebneri 'Leonard Messel'

the centre of each is a bunch of brilliant red stamens. This is a very striking shrub.

Mahonia

We have here an invaluable group of evergreen shrubs, and apart from their attractive holly-like green leaves, they have the considerable merit of flowering during the dull winter months. Ranging in size from low-growing ground cover types to others reaching 7 – 8 ft (2 – 2.4 m) in height, *Mahonia* can be described as fairly hardy, although in very cold weather the leaves can get slightly damaged. Sun or shade, they are not too fussy, but under very heavy shade they can become rather drawn up and require added pruning. They are quite easy to propagate from late summer cuttings.

M. aquifolium (Oregon Grape)

This is an excellent, tough *Mahonia* native to the West Coast of the USA. The green shiny leaves have a distinctly bronze tinge which is more noticeable during the winter. The bunches of yellow flowers start in late winter and carry on well into the spring. Deep blue berries follow the flowers, and these are covered in a powdery bloom giving them a strong resemblance to small grapes.

As a ground-cover shrub this *Mahonia* is very useful, and under most conditions it will produce suckers and spread quite rapidly. If left unpruned it can become definitely untidy, so to achieve the best ground cover effect cut hard back after flowering. This *Mahonia* is best propagated from seed extracted from the autumn fruit, but cuttings will also root. There is a red-leaved selection called *M. a.* 'Atropurpurea', and a new free-flowering form called *M. a.* 'Apollo' is quickly gaining popularity.

109

M. 'Charity'

This is a superb shrub with finely cut, large holly-type leaves. Early in the winter it is covered in sprays of soft yellow flowers. Unlike the equally popular *M. japonica* which tends to hide the sprays of flower, on *M.* 'Charity' these appear as bunched sprays at the end of each stem. All *Mahonia* are quite happy to be pruned as required. *M.* 'Charity' can become rather tall and lanky, and a light prune after flowering does keep the bush in good shape.

M. japonica

The best known of all *Mahonia* species, *M. japonica* is winter-flowering with sprays of richly-scented, soft yellow flowers. In the past it has often been confused with *M. bealei*, which has rather smaller, upright spikes of yellow flowers. The majority of nurseries and garden centres now sell *M. japonica* with drooping flower sprays.

Some selective pruning can be carried out to keep the bush in shape. A few sprays of flower

Mahonia 'Charity'

mixed with the early *Iris stylosa* will make a lovely spring flower arrangement.

M. 'Lionel Fortescue'

As yet not so well known, this hybrid is again winter-flowering, producing long sprays of soft yellow flowers.

M. 'Undulata'

This variety has exceptionally attractive foliage which is the glossiest of them all. It grows up to 6 ft (1.8 m) in height with rich yellow flowers.

Myrtus (Myrtle)

M. communis, the common myrtle, is not hardy and therefore is only suitable for use in gardens in milder climates. Even then, it still requires a

110

Olearia × scilloniensis

---

sheltered corner or warm wall. It is a late-flowering, fragrant shrub which produces a mass of white fluffy flowers in the late summer. Myrtle can be clipped after flowering and will root easily from summer cuttings.

Olearia

This genus contains one or two useful shrubs that are very well suited to windblown seaside conditions in milder areas. Natives of Australia and commonly called the 'Daisy Bush', all are sun-lovers which will grow in most soils, thriving on chalk. They generally have silvery foliage with soft white down under the leaves. The flowers are like small white daisies, very similar to Michaelmas daisies. Many members of this family are prone to 'legginess' and require frequent spring pruning to retain a compact shape. Propagation is quite easy from summer cuttings.

O. × haastii

This species has small silvery leaves and a mass of white daisy flowers in mid-summer. Of all the *Olearia* species it is perhaps the hardiest and it can be useful in open, exposed situations.

O. macrodonta

Commonly called the 'New Zealand Holly', this species has handsome, bright green leaves with a definite holly-like shape. Bunches off scented white flowers appear in summer on this evergreen shrub that can eventually grow up to 10 ft (3 m) high. It is essential to prune, otherwise you will end up with a very gaunt-looking specimen.

O. × scilloniensis

Sadly, this species is not too hardy, because, as the name indicates, this fast-growing hybrid is native to the Isles of Scilly. In an open sunny position it makes a dense rounded shrub of silver-grey foliage. In late spring the whole bush is

111

completely covered in brilliant white daisy-like flowers, and it flowers with such profusion that the leaves disappear. This is a really beautiful shrub if you are lucky enough to be in a mild area. Prune to keep a compact shape, and also remove dead flowers after flowering.

Osmanthus

This genus comprises some useful evergreen shrubs, which thrive in almost any type of soil.

O. delavayi

Here we have a very handsome evergreen, with shiny green leaves resembling small holly leaves. A mass of fragrant white flowers, reminiscent of jasmine, appear in spring. This is a slow-growing shrub with an eventual height of 8 – 10 ft, (2.4 – 3 m) in favourable conditions. It is not totally hardy. It will propagate from cuttings taken in summer but be patient as results can be rather slow.

O. × burkwoodii

For many years this evergreen was known as × *Osmarea* 'Burkwoodii', but some botanical juggling has now brought it back to the *Osmanthus* genus. It has one great advantage over *O. delavayi* in that it is very much hardier, although not so handsome. As a dense evergreen producing a mass of white flowers in spring it is very useful, and both *Osmanthus* could produce an interesting, evergreen flowering hedge. *O. × burkwoodii* will root from semi-ripe summer cuttings, but it is slow and not always easy.

Parrotia

Native to Iran, and a member of the winter-flowering witch hazel family, *P. persica* is one of the very best autumn colouring shrubs, producing a brilliant display of crimson and gold on the beech-like leaves. On large specimens the bark flakes away, giving an interesting winter effect. Over the years a wide spreading shrub will develop, so allow plenty of space. Propagation is not too easy, but semi-ripe cuttings can be

encouraged to root with the aid of bottom heat.

Pernettya

Splendid berrying shrubs, *Pernettya* will only grow in moist acid soils, achieving an eventual height of 4 – 5 ft (1.2 – 1.5 m). They produce some of the most striking berries of any winter shrub, and fortunately they are not great favourites with the birds.

Small, spiky evergreen foliage and a mass of tiny white flowers in spring is followed by autumn berries varying in colour from white, pink, mauve, and bright scarlet almost to black. Unfortunately this is another of those unisexual shrubs with male and female on separate plants; it is therefore wise to plant one male *Pernettya* with about five females. Under ideal conditions the shrubs will spread via underground runners, and for the best crop of berries plant in a sunny position. Propagation is quite easy from summer cuttings. For the best colours choose from the following varieties.

P. mucronata

P.m. 'Bell's Seedling' – a self-fertilising form with extra large, dark red berries.
P.m. 'Cherry Ripe' – bright, cherry-red berries.
P.m. 'Lilacina' – lilac berries.
P.m. 'Pink Pearl' – pink berries.
P.m. 'White Pearl' – gleaming white berries, showing up very well in the winter.

Philadelphus (Mock Orange)

The name of this shrub is a matter of constant confusion as it still continues to be called *Syringa*, a name in fact that applied only to the lilacs. This is a problem which goes back many years to when *Philadelphus* was included with the lilacs.

Late spring to early summer is the time for *Philadelphus*. All have white to cream-coloured flowers, and many are sweetly scented, but not all. There are tall-growing giants up to 15 ft (4.5 m) in height, and charming dwarf forms growing up to 2½ ft (75 cm) maximum. There are golden-leaved and variegated forms which can be rather unsatisfactory. Out of flower the *Philadelphus* are no beauties, looking at best like a bunch of unexciting sticks, so careful placing among other shrubs is important.

Easy to grow without being too fussy about soil, light shade suits a number of the family and helps to preserve the flowers which can be over fairly quickly. Pruning every year immediately after flowering is essential, otherwise you will end up with a gaunt, untidy bush. All *Philadelphus* flower on previous year's growth, so prune in summer and any new growth in that year will yield next year's flowers. Propagation is easy from soft cuttings during summer, or hardwood cuttings inserted in the open ground will root.

P. 'Beauclerk'

Eventually growing up to 6 ft (1.8 m) in height and equally wide, this variety has very fragrant white flowers with a soft pink flush in the base. They can be as much as 3 in (7.5 cm) across.

P. 'Belle Etoile'

This is another 6 ft (1.8 m) shrub with a pronounced deep purple stain at the base of each single flower. It has a very sweet scent, and one of the best for a small garden.

P. 'coronarius'

Very tall, up to 12 ft (3.5 m). *P. coronarius* has creamy white exceptionally strong-scented flowers in early summer. It is really too large for many gardens.

P. coronarius 'Aureus'

This is an excellent shrub with delightful, creamy yellow foliage in the spring. Carefully placed it can be one of the most effective golden shrubs, although because of the lighter foliage the flowers can be rather lost. A position away from hot sun is advisable as the rather delicate leaves can be easily scorched. There is also a variegated form but this scorches so badly that it is really not worth growing.

Philadelphus 'Belle Etoile'

P. 'Manteau d'Hermine'

However small your garden you can fit in this little treasure. Small, creamy white, scented blossoms appear on a compact bush growing to a maximum of 2 – 3 ft (60 – 90 cm) in height.

P. microphyllus

The flowers of this species have a fresh, fruity smell very similar to that of pineapples. A native of the USA, this is a fairly slow-growing *Philadelphus* – it eventually forms a dense twiggy bush around 4 ft (1.2 m) in height.

P. 'Virginal'

This is definitely the most popular double-

flowered form, with large, pure white, scented flowers. Sadly it is an unattractive plant when not in flower, especially during the winter, so plant among other shrubs to hide the bare stems.

Phlomis

Phlomis fruticosa (Jerusalem Sage) is a useful low-growing evergreen for the front of a border. It has large grey/green leaves resembling those of sage, and interesting whorls of pale yellow flowers in late summer and early autumn. As a native of the Mediterranean, an open sunny position is essential. It is easy to propagate from summer cuttings.

Phormium

P. tenax has tough green sword-like leaves which are capable of withstanding wind and sea spray but not extreme cold. *P. tenax* 'Purpureum' is fairly hardy, but in general the genus is only suitable for mild areas. The rigid upright shape of the *Phormium* varieties appears somewhat strange, but used as feature plants in a tub they can be effective. Otherwise, considerable care is required to place them among less rigid shrubs.

Photinia

If you garden on chalky soil, here is an excellent substitute for the lovely *Pieris* shrubs with their brilliant red spring growth. Only in the past few years have the *Photinia* shrubs deservedly become popular. Two or three evergreen members of the family are of most garden value, eventually forming 6 – 8 ft (1.8 – 2.4 m) high and equally wide shrubs. Fairly fast-growing, some pruning is useful to keep the bushes in good shape and also to encourage the brilliant red young shoots which make this such a striking shrub. They are definitely worth trying as an interesting evergreen hedging plant. Propagation from cuttings is quite easy during late summer to early autumn.

Photinia × fraseri 'Red Robin'

P. × fraseri 'Red Robin'

Without any doubt this variety has the most brilliant scarlet red shoots of all this genus. A mature bush in late spring can be a very striking sight with massed, scarlet red shoots. As a young shrub *P. ×f.* 'Red Robin' will grow fairly fast, and some pruning is required to form a compact plant. If left unpruned you will get fewer and fewer red shoots. The new growth is fairly tough, and although severe frost will cut it back a few weeks later another flush will appear. In fact, there is usually some colour from spring to autumn.

P. × fraseri 'Robusta'

This variety has smaller leaves and is generally more delicate than *P. ×f.* 'Red Robin'. The new shoots start off red, turning to almost deep pink. Sprays of white flowers in the spring are not very significant.

Physocarpus

P. opulifolius 'Luteus' is a medium-sized, deciduous shrub grown for its clear yellow leaves. As with many yellow-leaved shrubs, it is at its best in spring and early summer, gradually turning green as the season progresses. Keep pruned to encourage plenty of new growth, and propagate by means of summer cuttings.

Pieris

If you have lime-free soil here is a really exciting group of shrubs. Over the past few years a number of excellent new varieties have become available, adding even greater interest. All *Pieris* associate very happily with rhododendrons and azaleas and require identical cool, peaty soil conditions. Their attraction is twofold. A number of them produce brilliant scarlet new shoots in the spring, sometimes with sprays of characteristic lily-of-the-valley type flowers. The new shoots, which sadly can be damaged by spring frosts, gradually fade to pink and finally pale green. The remaining varieties produce sprays of white, and pink to almost red lily-of-the-valley flowers. All are evergreen, with one attractive variegated form. As fairly slow-growing shrubs they generally require little pruning; if it is necessary, carried out during the spring it will do no harm.

All members of the genus appreciate light shade, and a tall canopy of trees will also keep off a degree or two of spring frost. Propagation from cuttings is quite easy; 2 – 3 in (5 – 7.5 cm) long tips of current season's growth in a peaty compost will root easily with the aid of some bottom heat.

P. floribunda

Probably the main claim to fame of this species is its toughness. It produces a mass of short, upright flower spikes, starting to flower at a very early age. It is a useful plant that is still widely grown, but considering all the *Pieris* available it has a certain lack of charm.

P. 'Forest Flame'

As a garden shrub this one has everything to recommend it. It is a compact, graceful evergreen producing a mass of brilliant red shoots early in the spring; these eventually turn pink, then yellow and finally green. It is a little shy with flowers but the glorious spring display of fire is really quite enough. Try to find a site with some shelter from frost and wind. A really outstanding plant!

P. formosa forrestii 'Jermyns'

This is a really beautiful *Pieris*, on which the new growth is pale orange in colour. The attraction is in the drooping racemes of flower; throughout the winter they are superb orange-brown sprays, whilst the spring display combining the white flowers and orange stems is really beautiful. Perhaps not quite so hardy, this is nevertheless one of the most attractive of all *Pieris*.

P. formosa forrestii 'Wakehurst'

This is another *Pieris* of outstanding quality, with 3 – 4 in (7.5 – 10 cm) long dark green glossy leaves which offset the strong, brilliant red shoots in spring. Perhaps not quite so hardy as *P.* 'Forest Flame', the larger leaves can be scorched in severe

Pieris 'Forest Flame'

winter weather, so it is equally important to give early spring shelter away from frost and wind. This is a fairly strong-growing shrub that may benefit from an occasional prune to keep a good compact shape. Well-established plants can flower quite freely with sprays of pure white lily-of-the-valley flowers, often combining with the red shoots to give a dramatic effect.

P. japonica

It is always exciting to see this fairly hardy species in full flower, sometimes as early as late winter. It eventually forms a large evergreen bush up to 8 ft (2.4 m) in height, with sprays of hanging white

Pieris formosa forrestii 'Jermyns'

Pieris japonica 'Dorothy Wyckoff'

flowers which escape all but the most extreme cold weather.

P. japonica 'Blush'

This variety offers very pretty sprays of deep pink flowers which show up well against the dark green foliage. Many of the pink-flowered *Pieris* are recent introductions and certainly add great variety to the genus. This is not a very strong grower.

Pieris formosa forrestii 'Wakehurst'

P. japonica 'Dorothy Wyckoff'

A very recent introduction, this has extremely attractive red/brown buds which look colourful all through the winter, and leaves which are exceptionally glossy with an occasional tinge of purple. It is a very free-flowering and attractive *Pieris*.

P. japonica 'Flamingo'

The darkest of all, this variety has flowers which are really deep purple. It is still fairly new and will no doubt become very popular.

P. japonica 'Pink Delight'

This is an excellent name for a charming plant. It features sprays of delicate hanging flowers, and is a fairly strong grower.

P. japonica 'Variegata'

This is an exceptionally attractive variegated evergreen, a slow-growing dense shrub with a mass of small green leaves edged with white. The new growth is a delicate pale pink. Not a fast-growing plant, but excellent for woodland planting in light shade; in fact if planted in open sun it will flower quite profusely but the white sprays rather detract from the main beauty of the foliage.

P. taiwanensis

Quite happy in sun or light shade, this is a very free-flowering tough *Pieris*. It eventually grows to a maximum of around 6 ft (1.8 m), making it a very good shrub for a small garden, with very long erect sprays of flower in spring.

Pittosporum

There are a number of useful evergreen shrubs or small trees in this genus. Under ideal conditions they can achieve 30 – 40 ft (9 – 12 m) in height. Not too hardy, they are best suited to milder areas. An open, well-drained site with some shelter from cold winds is most suitable. The common green

Pittosporum is always popular with flower arrangers; the small shiny leaves contrast with the black stems and last a long time in water. Also in milder areas the green can make an excellent hedge.

All *Pittosporum* will tolerate pruning; they are not fast-growing but some control may be necessary to keep a compact shrub. Certain varieties flower profusely in late spring and early summer. The flowers are fairly insignificant, deep purple in colour, but what they lose in appearance they more than make up for with an exquisite honey-like scent.

P. tenuifolium

Propagation is best done by seed, which is exceptionally sticky when collected. Mix it with a little sand to separate the seeds, and it germinates quite easily. For the variegated and gold forms try summer cuttings with bottom heat – but it is not too easy.

P. tenuifolium 'Garnetti'

There is a charming combination of colours in this variety. Added to the silver leaves with white margins is a pink flush that is most noticeable during the winter.

P. tenuifolium 'Silver Queen'

This is a very light shrub with silvery grey leaves margined with white. It certainly needs a sheltered site.

P. tenuifolium 'Tom Thumb'

This is a fairly new introduction, native to New Zealand, the home of many *Pittosporum*. It appears to grow to around 3 ft (90 cm) making a thick dome-shaped bush. The foliage is an interesting combination of deep purple-red with pale green, shiny new growth.

P. tenuifolium 'Warnham Gold'

This is a very bright shrub, which has a mass of

Pittosporum tenuifolium 'Garnetti'

shiny evergreen leaves; the new leaves start greenish-yellow and when mature become a shiny golden yellow.

Potentilla

Over the past few years, new shrubby varieties of *Potentilla* have been appearing thick and fast, and it has now become quite difficult to select the very best. These shrubs have two strong points to recommend them: they are completely hardy and they flower continually during the summer and well into the autumn. Hard autumn or spring pruning is essential to maintain a good bush, and to get the best flowers. During the winter months it appears as a very twiggy, dead-looking bush which is not the least attractive. For really easy-

Potentilla 'Goldfinger'

going shrubs, tolerant of all soils, *Potentilla* are probably unbeatable. Propagation is exceptionally easy from soft summer cuttings.

P. × dahurica 'Manchu'

This spreading shrub has grey foliage and white flowers, and is native to China.

P. 'Daydawn'

This is a variety with very attractive peach-pink flowers.

P. 'Goldfinger'

Many of the *Potentilla* have simple, pale yellow flowers, but *P.* 'Goldfinger' has an excellent compact habit with large golden yellow flowers.

P. 'Longacre'

This has pretty silver foliage with pale yellow flowers. It is a very prostrate variety that is commonly used as ground cover.

P. 'Red Ace'

This is an exciting new colour break, and under cool conditions the flowers are an intense orange to red. Unfortunately they fade in bright sunlight.

P. 'Royal Flush'

Again a new colour in the *Potentilla* genus, with pink flowers.

121

P. 'Sunset'

Rich orange flowers are a feature of this variety.

P. 'Tangerine'

Growing to a maximum of around 2 ft (60 cm), and forming a dense mound, the flowers are rich coppery yellow.

Prunus (including Flowering Cherries)

Here we have an exceptionally varied collection of useful shrubs with very varied characteristics. Firstly there are the deciduous, shrub-like flowering cherries, and secondly the cherry laurels which are all evergreen, with the common laurel being the most widely planted. There are also a number of useful deciduous shrubs in the *P. cerasifera* species (Cherry Plum).

P. cerasifera 'Pissardii'

To make a fairly unusual hedge the Cherry Plum is certainly worth considering. This deep purple-leafed *Prunus* is often seen as a shrub or small tree, and during the summer months it forms an attractive hedge with delicate pink spring flowers. It has recently become fashionable to plant a hedge mixing in the bronzy-green cultivar *P. c.* 'Trailblazer' of the bright green form *P. c.* 'Greenglow'. The mixed colours can produce an interesting, patchwork hedge. It can be propagated from cuttings.

P. glandulosa 'Albiplena'

It is odd that the Chinese Bush Cherry is not more popular. It is a charming rather upright growing shrub. In spring the branches are covered in small double white flowers. There is also a double pink flowered variety called *P.g.* 'Rosea Plena'. At one time both these lovely cherries were commonly grown under glass and sold as cut flowers. Plant in a sheltered position and prune hard after flowering.

P. laurocerasus (Cherry Laurel)

This is the vigorous evergreen that most of us know as laurel. It is quite an attractive plant, when kept in good condition; the leaves are bright and shiny all year round. It can form an excellent evergreen screen. The larger bushes flower very freely in spring, producing a mass of deep red to almost black cherry-like fruits in the autumn.

The most common use is to make an excellent dense evergreen hedge which, if cut carefully, can be very handsome (if you prune with shears this will cut all the leaves in half which is very ugly). It is a very greedy plant with spreading roots which extract all the nutrients for a considerable area around the plant, so keep it away from your favourite shrubs. Propagation is very easy from late summer to autumn cuttings.

P. laurocerasus 'Otto Luyken'

This is a rather rigid evergreen that is probably better suited to the more formal gardens of the continent. This is a dwarf form of the common laurel, eventually growing to around 4 ft (1.2 m) in height. The leaves are exceptionally glossy, green, narrow and pointed. As a fairly small plant *P. l.* 'Otto Luyken' will produce a mass of white candle-like flowers which are very attractive. It can be used to form a low, informal evergreen hedge, or alternatively pruned into a more formal shape. Propagation is easy from summer cuttings.

P. laurocerasus 'Zabeliana'

This is one of the best ground-cover laurels. Rarely growing more than 3 ft (90 cm) in height, it can achieve at least 12 ft (3.5 m) or more in width. Again a free-flowering laurel producing a good spring display of white flowers, it is easily propagated from summer cuttings.

P. lusitanica

This is a handsome evergreen, commonly called Portuguese Laurel, after its native land. It is tough, dense and not unattractive. If you want a good screen, plant individual specimens that will grow up to 20 ft (6 m) in height. As a hedging plant it is also very useful. Apart from attractive glossy green leaves it can be quite an effective flowering plant, producing a mass of creamy-white racemes of flower in early summer.

There is also an attractive variegated form of Portuguese Laurel called *P. l.* 'Marbled White', no doubt useful for the keen flower arranger, this cultivar is not quite so hardy. The *Prunus* shrubs are happy on nearly all garden soils, and are easily propagated from summer cuttings without the aid of heat.

P. tenella

This is a charming low-growing shrub, commonly called the Dwarf Russian Almond, and growing to a maximum height of around 4 ft (1.2 m). It will, under ideal conditions, occasionally set almond-like fruits. By far the best cultivar native to the Balkans is *P. t.* 'Fire Hill', in which little clusters of rosy red shoots cover the stems in spring. Try to find a sheltered site, because although the plant is quite hardy too exposed a position can damage the flowers. It can be propagated from summer cuttings, or layered. No pruning is necessary.

P. triloba

The double pink rosettes of this early-flowering cherry are seen at best when it is planted against a warm south wall. It will flower profusely as soon as early spring. This is another charming plant that has been extensively forced under glass for the cut flower trade. Immediately after flowering, prune hard back to encourage new growth to flower next year. It can be planted in a shrub border but against a wall it really is seen at its best. Propagate from summer cuttings, but beware of grafted plants which can produce a mass of suckers.

Pyracantha (Firethorn)

Here is a genus that offers almost everything you could ask of a garden shrub. They are hardy, growing easily and fast on all garden soils. The spring display of white flowers is perhaps not spectacular, but the red, orange or yellow berries that make up the autumn show are certainly outstanding. Added to all these assets it is a very flexible plant. Apart from hedging the most common position for *Pyracantha* is against a house wall or fence. It is happily pruned into any shape, and will grow on any aspect including north, adding to its value as a wall plant. A *Pyracantha* will also grow happily as an independent shrub, making a large thick semi-evergreen bush. A wide variety of birds also favour this plant; late in the autumn there is usually a battle to save the berries, and a spray with one of the proprietary bird repellents will usually help. Semi-ripe cuttings of current season's growth 2 – 3 in (5 – 7.5 cm) long, will root quite easily during summer. Being vigorous, pruning is essential; this must be carried out carefully after flowering and the art is to keep the plant under control but to avoid cutting off any berries.

Pyracantha varieties do suffer from two unfortunate maladies. The more common is scab, which is evident from a sooty mould all over the plant. To control this, spray with Captan two or three times in spring and again during summer. Less common is the more serious complaint of fireblight which is characterised by persistent die-back on certain stems. If this becomes prevalent the only course of action is to dig up and burn the affected plant.

P. 'Alexander Pendula'

This plant has an intense, weeping habit, and is useful as a ground-cover shrub. Alternatively if encouraged up to 4 – 5 ft (1.2 – 1.5 m) by tying it to a cane and then allowing it to weep, it could make a lovely weeping shrub. The flowers and consequent berries are not as profuse as in other *Pyracantha* varieties.

P. 'Mohave'

A number of new varieties of *Pyracantha* has resulted from breeding work carried out in the USA. This vigorous cultivar is certainly one of the best and has been specially produced to resist disease. It has rather larger dark green leaves and flowers very freely, producing a crop of large, deep orange berries. It is certainly the best type for hedging purposes.

P. 'Orange Charmer'

The berries of this variety are pale orange, but very large and profuse. It is certainly an excellent *Pyracantha*, adding to the colour range.

P. 'Orange Glow'

This really has such a good name that it could scarcely fail to be successful. It has quite small shiny leaves on a fairly upright plant, and a mass of bright orange berries in the autumn.

P. 'Soleil d'Or'

With its attractive crop of yellow berries, this is not quite such a vigorous variety, but planted among the red and orange berries it adds another attractive colour.

P. 'Variegata'

This is a variegated *Pyracantha* which is certain to find favour with some enthusiasts. Nevertheless, it can be a rather sickly plant, missing many of the best features of the genus.

Rhododendron

Here we have a fascinating genus, ranging from giant specimens up to 40 ft (12 m) high, down to the miniature ground-hugging alpine varieties.

There are in the region of 1,000 wild varieties of rhododendron, and no doubt more to be discovered. They are mainly plants of the northern hemisphere. The greatest number of varieties are found among the mountains of South West China, through the border area with Tibet and Burma in the Assam and Nepal. A very few rhododendrons grow in Northern Siberia, but the significance of these is the connection via Alaska with the rhododendron population of North America. This extends right across Canada and down through the United States both by the west coast to California and via the eastern region to the Gulf of Mexico. The species, *Rhododendron ferrugineum* (or more commonly 'Alpine Rose'), grows in the eastern Alps of Europe.

Over the past years many new low-growing rhododendrons have been introduced, far more suited to modern compact gardens. This allows the owner of a small garden to enjoy a wider range of these beautiful evergreen plants.

To grow rhododendrons successfully is quite easy if the conditions are right. Basically there are three requirements as follows.

a) The soil must be acid or, at the very least, neutral, containing no lime. The pH scale used to measure soil acid/alkaline levels should ideally read from a low of pH 5 up to around 6.5 or perhaps 7. Above a 7 reading, rhododendrons will not grow happily, and unless something can be done to reduce this figure (as described on p.15) it would be wise not to try rhododendrons at all.

b) Plenty of moisture is essential. In moist, high rainfall, coastal areas they will really thrive. In drier areas, plenty of mulching with peat, bark or spent hops, plus extra water in the dry summer months, will be necessary.

c) Temperature is another important factor, because many of the more beautiful rhododendrons will not survive the extremes of a cold winter. Fortunately there are many rhododendron hybrids which have been developed to tolerate the extreme temperatures of Europe, N. America and Scandinavia.

So, for optimum results, acid soil, high rainfall and a mild climate are required.

Rhododendrons are shade-loving plants, giving their best performance under light dappled (not heavy) shade. Do not plant too near large trees as these will take out too much moisture during the summer months. Apart from offering cool moist soil conditions, with a high humus content of leaf mould or peat which these shallow rooted plants love, light shade has the added advantage of giving some protection from cold spring weather which can so easily damage the first blooms.

In a mild winter we can expect the first flowers in mid-winter with a succession of varieties giving colour right through to late summer. The early-flowering varieties require the most protected position away from cold, wind and frost. As we progress in to late spring with the advent of warmer weather many rhododendrons will thrive in fully exposed positions.

As a fairly slow-growing plant, pruning is seldom necessary. If a plant should grow too large or into a poor shape it will respond well to light pruning in spring. Sometimes very old plants require more drastic cutting back, and in the majority of cases they will grow away again into a dense, compact bush.

When you first buy and plant your young rhododendron allow a year or two for the plant to become established; flowering initially may be rather disappointing. Look on this plant as a long-term investment that will, in time, give colour for many years.

Propagation of the large-leaved rhododendron is not easy, yet with improved techniques many can be rooted from cuttings 4 – 5 in (10 – 12.5 cm) long taken in autumn. Traditionally, many rhododendrons have been grafted onto the wild *Rhododendron ponticum,* which accounts for the occasional suckers. In many old and overgrown gardens it is common to see the original colourful hybrid completely taken over by the more vigorous mauve-flowered *R. ponticum* suckers. If they do appear, cut or tear them off at the earliest possible stage. For the keen amateur, layering is an interesting method of propagating a few rhododendrons (see p.37).

Many of the dwarf rhododendrons do in fact root quite easily from semi-ripe cuttings inserted into an open rooting medium with peat and perlite; extra bottom heat will speed up the process but is not always essential.

Uses range from tall screens, evergreen hedges and ground cover to interesting foliage and bark. A few rhododendrons have exquisite scent plus, of course, a wide range of flower shapes and colours. Here is something for everyone, subject to having the correct growing conditions.

Rhododendron hardiness

To express the degree of hardiness the symbol H has been used, with the numbers 1 – 4 representing the degree. H4 indicates a very hardy plant that will grow in fairly cold areas and tolerate sun or shade. H3 requires a more sheltered site. H1 or H2 are for frost-free gardens, or suitable only for the conservatory.

Dwarfs

Ideal for the small garden, the dwarf range covers plants growing ultimtely to 1 – 3 ft (30 – 90 cm) high.

R. 'Carmen' H4

The ultimate height of this dwarf treasure is about 1 ft (30 cm). It has small shiny green leaves and a display of deep scarlet waxy flowers. This is an ideal plant for the small garden and can be planted in a rock garden. To get the best amount of flower a fairly open, light position is best. It will root fairly easily from cuttings taken in autumn. It is fairly slow-growing.

R. 'Cilpinense' H4

A delightful plant, one of the first to show colour in the early spring. *R.* 'Cilpinense' forms a well-rounded compact bush. The flowers are large and bell-shaped, up to 2½ in (6 cm) across. The pale pink flowers turn almost to white as they fade. As this variety flowers so early it is essential to find a sheltered site in the garden. It will root easily from semi-ripe cuttings in the autumn.

R. 'Creeping Jenny' H4

This is a low-growing form of the very popular *R.* 'Elizabeth'. With a final height of 2 – 3 ft (60 – 90 cm) this is another excellent plant for the small garden. It has clusters of brilliant scarlet flowers that are larger than you would expect on such a low-growing plant, and produces a mass of scarlet early in the spring but can be caught by late frost. It is very easy to root from cuttings in the autumn.

R. 'Curlew' H4

The soft yellow flowers have red-brown marking in the throat. This low-spreading dwarf rhododendron is a fairly new and welcome introduction.

R. impeditum H4

This excellent shrub is found high in the

125

mountains of South China at around 15,000 ft (5,000 m). From such a wild mountain site it is obviously rough and low-growing, and again is a possible candidate for the rock garden. Small grey/green leaves make this a plant of interest at all times of the year, even when the purplish-blue flowers have finished their spring display. In addition, planted *en masse* it can act as excellent ground cover. Being a plant that thrives in the high mountain country, it prefers an open site in the garden. It is fairly easy to root from cuttings in the autumn.

R. 'Phalarope' H4

This is an excellent medium height rhododendron for the small garden achieving a final height of around 3 ft (1 m). The colour of the flowers is an unusual soft lavender. For many weeks during the spring this rhododendron is a mass of colour.

R. 'Pink Drift' H4

This is another possibility for the rock garden. It is a dense, low-growing plant with tiny aromatic silver-grey leaves. It flowers very freely around mid-spring, with a profusion of soft lavender flowers, and is easy to root from semi-ripe cuttings.

R. 'Princess Anne' H4

A very welcome addition to the dwarf hybrid rhododendrons, this variety forms a dense low bush with small green leaves, often tinged with a bronze-copper colour, especially in the winter months. A mass of pale yellow flowers in late spring contrasts well with the more common pinks, reds and blues. It is fairly easy to root from autumn cuttings.

R. 'Ptarmigan' H3

This dwarf rhododendron has a habit of spreading out in a dense mat. It is quite an early-flowering variety, which will require a sheltered spot if you are to avoid damage from frost and wind. The simple flowers are single and white with pronounced brown stamens in the centre.

Medium-growers

This covers the range of rhododendrons which grow 3 – 10 ft (1 – 3 m) in height.

R. 'Bambi' H4

Bambi has inherited the excellent compact habit from its parent, *R. yakushimanum*. It flowers late in the spring and is quite happy growing in full sun. The flowers are an unusual combination of deep and pale orange; when in full flower, the bush is totally covered in colour, hiding all the leaves. This variety can be rooted from late summer to early autumn cuttings, but it is not easy.

R. 'Blue Diamond' H4

Fairly slow-growing, eventually reaching about 4 – 6 ft (1.2 – 1.8 m) in height, this is one of the best and hardiest of spring-flowering blue rhododendrons. It is a reliable plant that will thrive both in the open and light shade. A mass of lavender-blue flowers cover the bush each spring, a useful colour that contrasts well with some of the early-flowering yellow rhododendrons. It is easy to root from late summer cuttings.

R. 'Bow Bells' H4

This is an excellent name to describe the beautiful shell-pink large bells that cover this plant in late spring. It is a compact plant with interesting, round-shaped leaves which are attractive throughout the year. The new spring growth is a pleasant coppery colour. It is fairly easy to root from late summer cuttings.

R. 'Britannia' H4

This really old favourite from Holland forms a dense low plant, growing to a maximum of about 8 ft (2.4 m). The foliage is an olive-green colour which shows up the bright scarlet flowers. Flowering generally late in the spring, which avoids any late frost, it will grow quite happily in a fairly open site. It is very difficult to propagate from cuttings, and is generally grafted onto *R. ponticum;* so keep a close watch for suckers.

R. catawbiense H4

From the Catawba River in North Carolina, USA, this is perhaps a rhododendron that will not win any prizes for flower quality, but it makes up for this in being exceptionally hardy, apparently able to withstand up to 60 degrees of frost. It forms a low, dense bush, 8 – 10 ft (2.4 – 3 m) high. It is late-flowering, with round trusses of lilac-purple flowers. There are various forms, including a white one, and all are quite easy to root from cuttings in the autumn.

R. 'Christmas Cheer' H4

This one falls between medium and large in size. It is certainly a compact rhododendron that generally grows to a maximum of 6 ft (1.8 m). In a mild season it can be one of the first to come into flower, with light trusses starting deep pink in bud and gradually fading. Because it blooms so early, some light shade will protect the flowers from frost.

R. 'Elizabeth' H3 – 4

This must be one of the most widely planted medium rhododendrons of all time, with thoroughly deserved popularity. It grows to a medium height of 4 – 5 ft (1.2 – 1.5 m), growth is fairly fast compared to that of many rhododendrons and it forms a round dense mass of a bush. *R.* 'Elizabeth' puts on a brilliant display of colour each year with a mass of waxy scarlet bells in the spring. It always appears so eager to flower that buds can appear on very small plants only 1 ft (30 cm) high. It is an easy shrub to grow and has the added advantage of being quite easy to root from cuttings in the summer.

R. 'Fabia' H3 – 4

This is a great favourite with delightful, soft orange flowers in late spring to early summer. Flowering quite late in the spring, in fact almost early summer, it helps to extend the season of rhododendrons in flower. It is fairly easy to root from cuttings taken in the summer to early autumn. The grey-green foliage and pale orange flowers make this a marvellous rhododendron to cut for indoor decoration.

R. 'Golden Torch' H4

As the name implies here is a yellow-flowered hybrid which is hardy and suited to the small garden. This again is a hybrid from the prolific *R. yakushimanum,* which features good green foliage and trusses of clear yellow bell-shaped flowers late in the spring. Grafting is the most common method of propagation.

R. 'Hotei' H3 – 4

From the USA, this rhododendron has deep yellow trusses of flowers which appear late in the spring. It is a fairly slow-growing variety, but certainly worth trying for the unique yellow of the flowers.

R. 'Humming Bird' H3

This has beautiful single deep red waxy bells on a dense green bush growing eventually to 4 – 5 ft (1.2 – 1.5 m) in height. To see this lovely rhododendron in full flower is quite a sight. The leaves are small, round and very dark green sometimes almost looking black. Even when not in flower it forms quite an attractive bush, and is fairly easy to root from cuttings in the autumn.

R. 'May Day' H3

The flowers really glow on this compact bush with an intense orange to red brilliance. It is fairly quick-growing and free-flowering, with colour late in the spring.

R. 'Pink Cherub' H4

This is more vigorous than *R.* 'Bambi', but still

retains a fairly compact habit from the parent *R. yakushimanum*. Large trusses of pink flowers appear late in the spring, and the grey-green foliage is fairly distinctive. Young plants are generally grafted onto *R. ponticum,* as this one can be difficult to root.

R. 'Praecox' H4

The name 'Praecox' means 'early', and this variety certainly lives up to its name, being one of the very first to produce rosy-lilac flowers just as winter moves into spring. It grows 4 – 8 ft (1.2 – 2.4 m) high, and when surrounded by groups of the early flowering narcissi it provides a delightful splash of colour early in the year. With such an early-flowering shrub, frost and bad weather can ruin the flowers, so try to find a sheltered spot in the garden. It is fairly easy to grow from cuttings taken late summer to early autumn.

R. 'President Roosevelt' H3

Here is certainly a strange member of the rhododendron genus that will not fail to attract attention. This is one of the very few variegated rhododendrons; the dark green leaves are splashed in various shades of gold and yellow, giving interest all the year round. The flowers are equally unusual with a light pink base shading to almost red, and a marked frilly edge to each individual flower. To get the best variegated effect, plenty of light is necessary. Not too easy to root, it is best layered or grafted.

R. racemosum H4

This is a delightful species, a native of Western China where it is found growing high in the mountains. Stems on the new growth have bright red bark with leaves distinctly grey-green in colour. They are aromatic when crushed and after spring rain on a warm day give off a pungent scent. In spring the whole bush is a mass of small pale to deep pink flowers growing up and down the stem. This is one rhododendron that certainly does need to be pruned fairly frequently,

otherwise it can develop into a straggly bush. It is not an easy plant to grow from cuttings, but it germinates well and grows easily from seed. There is also a white-coloured form available.

R. 'Rotenburg' H4

From Germany originates this very tough rhododendron with enormous creamy-yellow flowers. An added bonus are the very shiny green leaves which give interest throughout the year. The ultimate height of this shrub is about 8 – 10 ft (2.4 – 3 m). It will root from cuttings but is not at all easy.

R. 'Scarlet Wonder' H4

This is a reliable and very tough hybrid bred in Germany and therefore able to stand very cold weather. It grows into a mound of shiny dark green leaves which offset the scarlet flowers during late spring. This is a first-class low-growing shrub for any small garden, eventually growing to a maximum of 4 ft (1.2 m). If planted in groups, it can make excellent ground cover. It is easy to root from cuttings during late summer to early autumn.

R. schlippenbachii H3

A deciduous rhododendron that is worth growing for its name alone, this is a native of East Korea and was discovered in 1854 by Baron Schlippenbach. The leaves are exceptionally attractive and delicate, with a pronounced red flush early in the season. Charming, soft pink flowers appear in middle to late spring. A large shrub or clump of this rhododendron in full flower is really a memorable sight. Try to choose a sheltered site away from spring frost which can damage both leaves and flowers. Propagation is best from seed.

R. 'Seven Stars' H4

Over the past 10 – 15 years, numerous new rhododendrons have been introduced by various plant breeders. By far, one of the most prolific parents has been that delightful species from

Japan, *R. yakushimanum*. *R.* 'Seven Stars' is one of the many offspring of this plant and is definitely a shrub with a great future, especially for the smaller garden. Flowering around the middle of spring, the lovely bell-shaped flowers, with a fairly distinct frilly edge, start deep pink in bud changing to white with a faint pink flush. It forms a good compact plant with attractive dark green foliage, growing to a maximum of around 8 ft (2.4 m) in height. It may be a difficult one to root from cuttings.

R. 'Souvenir of W.C. Slocock' H4

This is an excellent plant for the small garden, with a dense compact habit eventually growing to around 8 ft (2.4 m) in height. The opening buds are a lovely apricot colour with the large trusses of flower opening to a creamy yellow flushed with pink. Flowering fairly late in the spring, it is fairly slow-growing. Propagation from cuttings in the autumn is possible, with the aid of additional bottom heat.

R. 'Temple Belle' H3

This forms a neat bush with attractive round leaves, and is a good compact plant for the small garden. Fairly free-flowering it has bell-like flowers, about 2 in (5 cm) long, deep pink with a waxy texture. It is quite an easy one to root from autumn cuttings.

R. 'Unique' H4

It is easy to identify this dense, low-growing variety by the characteristic neat round leaves. It grows to a maximum of around 8 ft (2.4 m) in height with attractive creamy-yellow flowers speckled in the throat with little red dots. It will happily grow in full sun where it flowers late in the spring, and will root from cuttings taken in early autumn with the aid of bottom heat.

R. vaseyi H4

The mountains of North Carolina are the home of this charming and very hardy plant. In many ways it resembles more a deciduous azalea but botanically is classed among the rhododendrons. The bushes can grow up to 6 ft (1.8 m) in height, but generally they are little more than half that. Very delicate pink butterly-like flowers cover the bushes in late spring, appearing before the foliage. This is a shrub that has great charm. In the autumn there are usually plenty of seed pods, and this is the best method of propagation.

R. williamsianum H4

At all times of the year this is an attractive, low-growing rhododendron. Delicate, small round leaves about 1 in (2.5 cm) long provide an interesting contrast to any associated plants. The flower buds are a deep sealing-wax red to brown, and open into single pale pink bells. The new spring growth is an attractive bronze-green, but unfortunately it is easily damaged by spring frost. This excellent species is an exciting shrub that has also been widely used by hybridisers to produce plants such as *R.* 'Bow Bells', *R.* 'Temple Belle', *R.* 'Humming Bird' and *R.* 'Moonstone'. It is fairly easy to root from late summer cuttings.

R. 'Winsome' H3

This is an interesting combination of rather hairy copper-red foliage, especially on the young shoots, and deep pink pendent flowers produced in great profusion, which are 2 – 3 in (5 – 7.5 cm) long and bell-shaped. This is an attractive shrub flowering late in the spring. It is easy to propagate from autumn cuttings, and fairly quick-growing. It will grow in full sun but can get damaged in extremely cold weather.

R. yakushimanum H4

Here is a magnificent rhododendron species that I would place very high on the list for any garden large or small. It is found on the island of Yakushima off the southern tip of Japan, growing high in the mountains. This hardy plant has a very compact habit, making it such an excellent small garden plant. The foliage is dark green and very shiny, but underneath every leaf is attractive furlike down which starts off white on the new leaves, turning with age to a darker suede-like brown. It is not a fast-growing plant, having an eventual height of 3 – 4 ft (90 – 120 cm). The flowers, which are surprisingly large for such a compact plant, start off deep pink, paling almost to white as it opens fully. It is one of the very useful rhododendrons that will thrive in light shade or an open position. Fortunately it also flowers late in the spring, avoiding the cold weather.

The majority of young plants are grafted onto *R. ponticum.* It will root from late summer cuttings, but is slow to grow into a larger plant.

Apart from being an excellent species it has been widely used by hybridisers to produce a race of excellent plants for the small garden.

Large growers

Among the larger-growing rhododendrons there is a bewildering number to choose from. They are all fairly slow-growing but under ideal conditions can over the years grow up to 20 – 30 ft (6 – 9 m) in height; careful placing is therefore essential. Many of the well known varieties have been around for approaching 100 years. Around the turn of the century new species were being discovered in various parts of the world which prompted a great deal of activity among the plant breeders, and these hardy evergreen shrubs with enormous pink, red and white flowers created quite a sensation in the gardening world.

Today, many of these old hardy hybrids which are generally tough and flower late in the spring are still the most popular varieties. I have listed a selected number which cover a wide spectrum of colour. The larger hybrids are generally about three years old when purchased and may take another two or three years before they really start giving a profusion of flower, even when mature. Good and bad flowering years are inevitable and this is probably governed by levels of rainfall and sunshine.

With improved methods of propagation, many

Rhododendron yakushimanum

130

of the larger rhododendrons are rooted from autumn cuttings, but a proportion are still grafted onto *R. ponticum* stocks, so look out for suckers.

R. 'Alice' H4

R. 'Alice' has a distinctive upright habit on a fairly fast-growing bush. It has obviously pointed leaves, and very large, pale pink flowers with a pale pink throat.

R. augustinii H3

This is a really lovely species that grows wild in central and west China. As a change from the usual large-leafed red and pinks, it is definitely one of the best blue rhododendrons. It eventually forms a bush 10 – 12 ft (3 – 3.6 m) high, with fairly narrow leaves 2 – 3 in (5 – 7.5 cm) long. In late spring this very free-flowering plant is a breathtaking mass of blue flowers splashed with yellow in the throat. Seedling forms have been grown of *R. augustinii* but it is important to obtain the best deep blue form for a striking display. A fairly easy one to root from cuttings, it also grows reasonably quickly, ideally in light shade with plenty of humus.

R. 'Blue Peter' H4

With large, dark green, very leathery leaves, this is a very vigorous plant, flowering late in the spring, with huge trusses of cobalt-blue flowers which have a distinctive frilly edge. The blue flowers are lighter in the throat which is marked with small red dots.

R. 'Cunningham's White' H4

This is perhaps not the most exciting rhododendron, with its medium trusses of white flowers late in the spring. It is however, an exceptionally hardy plant and very easy to root from cuttings. It is a useful flowering evergreen to plant as a screen, or clipped to form a thick hedge. *R.* 'Cunningham's White' is related to the purple-flowered *R. ponticum* that grows like a weed in many deciduous woods.

R. 'Cynthia' H4

First put on exhibition in 1862, this is one of the most vigorous and eventually tallest of all the hardy hybrids, attaining at least 25 ft (7.6 m) and under ideal conditions even more. With enormous trusses of deep pink flowers late in the spring, it is an excellent evergreen to form a large screen; but the flower colour has a strong hint of magenta which does not mix too easily with other colours. *R.* 'Cynthia' roots quite readily from autumn cuttings.

R. 'Doncaster' H4

This is another hardy old rhododendron, forming a thick dense shaped shrub up to 8 ft (2.4 m) in height. The foliage is a very dark green in colour. It is one of the more free-flowering rhododendrons, producing a mass of crimson/scarlet flowers late in the spring. With special care and bottom heat in the propagator, this rhododendron will root from cuttings. As a variety that produced flower buds even when quite small, *R.* 'Doncaster' has been used at times as a flowering pot-plant.

R. 'Fastuosum Flore Pleno' H4

Another tall-growing vigorous hybrid that has been available for well over 100 years, this one has attractive dark green foliage with a useful habit of flowering late in the spring, and even in early summer. The fairly loose trusses of rather unusual double flowers could be described as blue in colour, but a more accurate assessment would be bluish-mauve with pronounced green markings in the throat. This is another rhododendron that will root easily from cuttings.

R. 'Goldsworth Yellow' H4

There is always a good demand for yellow rhododendrons, especially late-flowering varieties that avoid spring frosts. This one forms a moderate-sized bush with apricot-pink buds that

Rhododendron augustinii

Rhododendron 'Hawk Crest'

open to clear yellow. Many of the more delicate yellows require light shade, but 'Goldsworth Yellow' appears to be quite happy in full sunlight.

R. 'Gomer Waterer' H4

One of the last to flower in the early months of summer; this is a handsome, tough plant with large leathery leaves and a very compact habit. The large flowers are striking, especially as the buds begin to break; they are mainly white, with a faint lavender tinge to the edges and a distinctive yellow-brown flash inside the flower. It is an excellent hardy hybrid.

R. 'Hawk Crest' H3

Of all the yellow-flowered hybrids, this is undoubtedly still one of the very best. Unfortunately, it is not the hardiest of rhododen-

drons, but can be seen at its best in light woodland under high oak trees. It forms a very open bush, producing very few flowers for the first year or two. Once established, it will flower quite freely, with deep orange buds opening to clear yellow flowers. Very difficult to propagate, the occasional cutting will root, but most plants of this uncommon rhododendron are produced from grafts onto the wild *R. ponticum*.

R. Loderi 'King George' H3

This is a giant among the rhododendrons. It has 9 – 12 flowers, which form an enormous open truss, and are very delicate shades of white flushed with pink. As an added bonus, there is the exquisite scent not normally associated with

Rhododendron Loderi 'King George'

---

rhododendrons. Large specimens of 18 – 20 ft (5.5 – 6 m) are not unusual, so plenty of space is essential. There are a number of other hybrid forms of *R.* Loderi, but 'King George' is certainly the most outstanding. The most common method of propagation is by grafting onto *R. ponticum* stocks, as it is not easy to root from cuttings.

R. 'Loder's White' H3

Enormous trusses of pure white flowers are produced on this magnificent rhododendron. There is a hint of pink when the buds first open, but this almost disappears when the flowers are fully open. It is quite a vigorous plant, eventually growing to 10 – 15 ft. (3 – 4.5 m) in height. Flowering late in the spring, *R.* 'Loder's White'

will grow in full sunshine, but such delicate flowers appreciate light shade. Not too easy to propagate, it will root from cuttings, but grafting is probably the most common method used.

R. 'Lord Roberts' H4

This tough old favourite has been available since 1900. The flowers are dark crimson with a flare of dark spots inside, and these show up well against the very dark green foliage. It is a fairly free-flowering rhododendron appearing late in the spring and eventually forming a medium sized bush, and is quite easy to root from cuttings in the autumn.

R. 'Moser's Maroon' H4

Rather akin to *Pieris* or *Photinia*, this hardy hybrid produces a flush of dark red shoots during

135

late spring and early summer. A fast growing, late flowering plant, its very deep maroon-red flowers can almost be lost among the deep red shoots. It can be pruned quite regularly to encourage the colourful new growth.

R. 'Mrs. G.W. Leak' H4

The very striking flowers make this rhododendron appear to be very alert. It has large pink conical trusses of flower up to 12 in (30 cm) high, with pronounced brown and crimson markings inside the flower. In full flower it would be difficult to ignore this plant.

R. 'Naomi' H4

A strong-growing plant happy in full sun or light shade, for the small garden it requires plenty of space, growing to 15 ft (4.5m) high and above, and almost as wide. The leaves are slightly round and grey-green in colour. Very large trusses of flower, with wide single florets are produced in a delicate pink with a touch of yellow, with the bonus of a delicious fragrance. If you have the space this is a beautiful shrub. Unfortunately, propagation is not easy, resulting in the majority being grafted onto *R. ponticum* stocks.

R. 'Purple Splendour' H4

This variety has genuine imperial purple flowers marked with a dark black flash in the throat. It is generally a fairly modest growing plant, eventually reaching around 10 ft (3 m). It has the further attraction of flowering late in the spring to almost early summer. It is certainly an interesting colour and ideal for the smaller garden, as well as being a free-flowering plant that will root from cuttings.

R. 'Queen Elizabeth II' H4

This is a fairly recent introduction flowering quite late in the spring, and in time should prove to be a

Rhododendron 'Mrs G.W. Leak'

really outstanding yellow rhododendron. It has already received two awards from The Royal Horticultural Society. It may prove difficult to propagate.

R. 'Wilgen's Ruby' H4

Good foliage and compact growth are two advantages of this popular hybrid. The leaves are an attractive olive-green colour which acts as an excellent background to the brilliant red flowers. As with most of the hardy hybrids, flowering is late in the spring, avoiding the usual cold winds and frost. This is an excellent small garden rhododendron growing ultimately to 8 – 10 ft (2.4 – 3 m). It will root from autumn cuttings with the aid of bottom heat.

Rhus

R. typhina (Stag's-horn Sumach) is rather a rangy shrub rising to a small tree. The young stems are covered in soft, brown down. This, coupled with the spikyness of the sparse stems, gives the stag's horn effect. The large frond-like leaves turn to glorious colours of red, orange and gold in the autumn. There is also an attractive cut-leaved form called *R. t.* 'Laciniata'. These shrubs have the habit of becoming gaunt if left unpruned, so in order to avoid bare leggy stems cut back hard in the early spring. The Sumachs have a common habit of sending up suckers; if lifted carefully these are the best means of producing new plants.

Ribes

It is the curiously pungent smell that makes *R. sanquineum*, the flowering currant, so distinctive. This is perhaps one of the most commonly grown flowering shrubs, reaching a maximum height of 5 – 6 ft (1.5 – 1.8 m). It grows fast and tolerates most soil conditions. In order to keep a good, compact shrub, it is essential to prune hard each year after flowering, and it can be used effectively as a flowering hedge. The widespread planting of the flowering currant is partly due to ease of propagation: softwood cuttings root happily in the summer, but it is even simpler to wait until the autumn and push a few hardwood cuttings in the open ground, which will generally be well-rooted by late spring. One of the best currants, with deep red flowers, is the cultivar *R. s.* 'Pulborough Scarlet'.

R. sanguineum 'Brocklebankii'

So many of the golden-leaved shrubs suffer damage from wind and weather, and this attractive currant is no exception. If you can find a sheltered site to suit the plant, it can be very effective, with pink flowers and light foliage.

Romneya

R. × hybrida 'White Cloud' can be a very difficult shrub to establish, but can then run riot, sending up suckers all over the place. Plant it in a well-drained loamy soil and try your luck. Be patient, because it can take a year or so to become established. The single, white poppy-like flowers with a central mass of yellow stamens are really beautiful. Try to plant it in a sheltered spot out of the wind.

Rosa

Shrub roses have great charm, a wide variety of habit and, in many cases, exquisite scent. (I have deliberately excluded the hybrid teas and floribundas from this section, as they will require a whole book of their own!) Sometimes you will hear the term 'old-fashioned' used for the shrub roses; to some extent this is quite apt, as many of the plants can be traced back many hundreds of years. For example, *R. alba, R. centifolia* varieties, moss roses, china roses, damask roses and *R. gallica* varieties all have a long history. Coming more up to date we have the splendid *R. rugosa* hybrids with handsome flowers and lovely autumn hips. At the beginning of the century the lovely free-flowering hybrid musk roses were developed and finally we now have an excellent selection of modern shrub roses which have added to the wonderful variety.

Greenfly, the number one insect pest on all roses, appear to keep clear of many shrub roses;

the dreaded black spot is also quite rare. A few can be attacked by mildew. If problems do arise use a systemic fungicide, based on the chemical Benomyl, to control mildew and black spot, and a pyrethrum-based insecticide to destroy the greenfly.

Another great advantage of the shrub roses is the ease of pruning; in fact very little is generally required. Any dead wood should obviously be removed, as well as any thin twiggy stems, and the last summer's shoots should be shortened by about half. If the bushes get too large and out of hand, they can be cut harder to keep a good shape.

Each spring try to give each plant a top dressing of rotted manure or compost and a light dressing of granular rose fertiliser; with these aids they will flower away happily for many years.

Many of the shrub roses will root quite easily from summer cuttings about 3 – 4 in (7.5 – 10 cm) long. Keep them in the pot or tray through the winter, pot them on the following spring and later that year they can be placed in the garden where they will quite quickly grow into flowering plants.

The full range of shrub roses is very large indeed; the following list contains a selection of the best.

R. alba 'Maxima'

This is a famous shrub rose that goes way back into history. Known as the 'Jacobite Rose' or 'White Rose of York', it has double white flowers up to 3 – 4 in (7.5 – 10 cm) across. This free-flowering, rather simple rose is very attractive.

R. alba 'Queen of Denmark'

Well over 100 years old, this is still a beautiful rose, quite vigorous-growing, finally reaching 5 – 6 f t (1.5 – 1.8 m). It has tight double flowers, which are soft pink with a button centre.

R. 'Ballerina'

This is quite low-growing with a final height of 4 ft (1.2 m). In early summer the whole plant is a mass of single pink clusters of flower.

R. 'Buff Beauty'

This is really quite a recent introduction in the world of shrub roses, arriving around 1920. It is a really excellent shrub, flowering on and off throughout the summer. It forms a fairly spreading bush of medium height with flowers borne in loose clusters. *R.* 'Buff Beauty' produces a mass of double apricot-yellow flowers.

R. 'Cecile Brunner' (Sweetheart Rose)

This one has perfectly-shaped soft pink flowers. The buds and flowers are just like a miniature hybrid tea flower. There are also bush and vigorous climbing forms.

R. centifolia muscosa (Moss or Old Cabbage Roses)

There is a certain nostalgia about these old moss roses; the name originates from the moss-like glands found on the sepals and flower stems. The very double flowers can hang down with their own weight, which means that they are not very well displayed on the bush. Heavy rain can also damage the blooms badly.

R. centifolia 'Fantin La Tour'

This is a real beauty with cupped, pale pink flowers shading to a deeper colour in the flower centre.

R. 'Cornelia'

The flower buds are deep salmon and open to clusters of soft pink double sprays of flower. It is low-growing.

R. 'Frühlingsgold'

This is a lovely hybrid. My only criticism of this plant is the eventual size and spread, which can be 8 – 10 ft (2.4 – 3 m). This can take up rather too much space. In flower, however, this large spreading bush is a magnificent sight. The large single yellow flowers appear in early summer. Sadly, there is not very much repeat flowering.

R. 'Frühlingsmorgen'

This is very similar to the above except that the single flowers are pink, shading to pale yellow in the centre.

R. gallica 'Versicolor' (Rosa Mundi)

The really striking flowers can best be described as white with extravagant red strips and streaks. This is a very old rose going back at least to the sixteenth century. It is rather a weak plant to grow.

R. 'Golden Wings'

With single clear yellow flowers with darker stamens, this is one of the most beautiful modern shrub roses.

R. 'Lady Penzance'

This rose has unique deep copper coloured single flowers, and is exceptionally fragrant. It is sadly often attacked by black spot and tends to form a rather thin, spindly bush. Even so it is worth persisting as the single flower is lovely.

R. 'Marguerite Hilling'

This is a deep pink sport of *R.* 'Nevada'. It is always a lovely summer sight, covered in deep pink single flowers.

R. 'Nevada'

This eventually forms a large bush 8 – 10 ft (2.4 – 3 m) with a rather weeping habit. The large single flowers are 4 – 5 in (10 – 12.5 cm) across, creamy white in colour often with a tinge of pink.

R. 'Nozomi'

This is a useful ground cover rose, growing almost flat on the ground and spreading over an area of about 3 – 4 ft (90 – 120 cm). It is not particularly vigorous and therefore can be very useful in a small garden. The flowers are pink fading almost to white.

R. 'Penelope'

The flowers are very soft salmon pink, and this variety can be used to form a flowering hedge.

R. rugosa 'Blanc Double de Coubert'

All the *R. rugosa* roses, apart from having a mass of lovely double or single flowers, have the added bonus of lovely red and orange hips in the autumn. This double white rose does get rather tall and leggy after a year or so. Hard pruning will help keep the plants in good shape.

R. rugosa 'Frau Dagmar Hastrup'

The simple pale pink single flowers are followed by an excellent display of hips in the autumn. It is a good shrub rose for the small garden as it rarely grows taller than 3 – 4 ft (90 – 120 cm).

R. rugosa 'Max Graf'

This is one of a number of ground-cover roses which can be usefully planted over manholes or down steep banks. It forms a vigorous spreading plant 2 – 3 ft (60 – 90 cm) high and about 8 – 10 ft (2.4 – 3 m) across. The whole plant is covered in dense glossy foliage and single, bright pink flowers.

R. rugosa 'Roseraie de l'Hay'

This is perhaps one of the most widely planted of all shrub roses, growing to a height of 5 – 6 ft (1.5 – 1.8 m). The fragrant double purple blooms are produced throughout the summer. It can be also used as a low screen or hedge which looks attractive in the autumn with all the colourful hips.

R. 'Scharlachglut' (Scarlet Fire)

The deep velvety red flowers are followed by a mass of red hips in the autumn.

Rosa 'Marguerite Hilling'

Rosa rugosa 'Max Graf'

Rosmarinus (Rosemary)

R. officinalis 'Miss Jessop's Variety'

A popular aromatic shrub that has been cultivated for many hundreds of years, this is a native of the hot, dry countries of the Mediterranean. As you might expect, it requires a dry, sunny position in the garden. This variety is one of the most popular, on account of the neat upright habit. The foliage is the familiar silver-grey, with pale blue flowers. It would be a mistake to describe rosemary as totally hardy, for it certainly can be damaged in a severe winter. Prune hard if the plant begins to get out of shape. It is an easy one to propagate from cuttings.

R. officinalis 'Severn Sea'

This lovely, free-flowering rosemary is certainly tender, but worth planting in a sunny, sheltered spot. The foliage is finer than the common *R. officinalis* and the flowers are very deep blue.

Rubus

R. Tridel 'Benenden' is an exceptionally beautiful, spring-flowering shrub with large, single white flowers and a central bunch of yellow stamens. The plant has a weeping habit with long arching branches which carry the simple flowers. Prune hard every year after flowering to encourage new growth.

Ruta

R. graveolens 'Jackman's Blue' is a little sub-shrub with intensely blue foliage. If you bruise a leaf between finger and thumb you get a very strange aromatic smell from its volatile oils. If you plant it in full sun and keep it trimmed, it can make an interesting blue mound in the garden. Root it from summer cuttings.

Salix

There are a number of dwarf willows which are rather neglected. *S. hastata* 'Wehrhahnii' is an exceptionally beautiful little willow that grows to an eventual height of 5 ft (1.5 m). Commonly called the 'Snow Pussy', it makes a lovely picture each spring, covered in a mass of silvery male catkins which show up well against the fresh green leaves. Soft or hardwood cuttings should root quite well.

Sambucus

S. nigra 'Aurea' is the golden version of the common elder which flowers and fruits so well in wild woods and hedgerows. The flowers have a strong, distinctive scent and are often collected to make a refreshing drink, and the berries later in the year can be used for elderberry wine. The golden-leaved form is a handsome garden shrub. It is vigorous and requires plenty of space. Even more attractive is the fern-leaved *S. nigra* 'Laciniata', commonly called the Parsley-leaved Elder, with finely-cut golden foliage. All this family respond well to pruning early in the spring to encourage new, bright-yellow foliage. Propagate from summer cuttings.

Sarcococca

S. confusa makes a neatly-formed plant reaching a maximum of 6 ft (1.8 m) in height. The white winter flowers are produced in sprays along every stem, and, as with so many winter-flowering shrubs, they have a very sweet scent, and one small sprig will perfume any room. After the flowers, there is a crop of handsome black berries. It is an easy subject to root from late-summer cuttings.

Senecio

It is interesting that the generic name of this New Zealand shrub is derived from the Latin word *senex* meaning 'old man' and refers to the grey foliage. The *Senecio* are not very hardy and need a sheltered, sunny site in the garden. *S. greyi* provides some of the best grey foliage of any garden shrub. It will eventually grow up to 8 ft (2.4 m) if left untended, and can become rather untidy. Prune annually, quite hard, to keep the shrub compact and to encourage plenty of the silver-grey foliage. The flowers are like bright-yellow daisies. It is quite easy to root from summer cuttings.

Skimmia

If you have a really gloomy corner in deep shade then one subject that will thrive there is a *Skimmia*. They are versatile, however, and can also grow happily in full sun and will thrive by the seaside. *S. japonica* has large, evergreen leaves and will eventually form a green mound about 3 ft (90 cm) high. Unfortunately, most of this genus are unisexual and have male flowers on one plant and female on another. Therefore, if you want brilliant red berries in the winter you must plant one male plant to every four or five females. It is an easy one to root from summer cuttings; and remember that cuttings will always be the same sex as the plant from which they are collected.

S. japonica 'Nymans'

This is one of the best female varieties, that will flower and fruit freely. Plant with the occasional male *Skimmia*, *S. japonica* 'Rubella' for example, to ensure a fine display of red winter berries.

S. japonica 'Rubella'

This is a fine male *Skimmia* which is well worth growing for the handsome scented flowers which are deep pink in bud opening soft pink. It has a distinctly upright habit of growth, best suited to an area of light shade to encourage the maximum number of flowers. In bloom, this is perhaps the most excellent of all *Skimmia* and, planted among a group of female varieties like the one above, it will give further satisfaction by causing them to produce a colourful crop of winter berries.

S. reevesiana

This charming little *Skimmia* was bred over 100

143

Skimmia japonica 'Rubella'

years ago in a nursery garden in Shanghai. It is a low-growing evergreen shrub rarely achieving a final height of more than 2 ft (60 cm). It has one big advantage over many other *Skimmia* species, in that it is bisexual and can produce berries as well as flowers on a single plant. *S. reevesiana* will not thrive where lime is present in the soil, as it prefers a rich acid loam.

Sorbaria

S. arborea is quite a handsome summer-flowering shrub, but it can grow up to 20 ft (6 m) in height and so could well be described as a space filler. The plumes of white flowers arrive late in the season, giving useful summer colour.

Spartium

S. junceum is the native Spanish broom of S. Europe. It forms a rather gaunt shrub with rush-like leaves growing eventually to about 9 – 12 ft

(2.7 – 3.6 m) in height. A mass of rich yellow flowers appear in the middle of summer when many shrubs have already faded. It is usually a shrub to plant in massed groups and will tolerate very dry conditions. The best way to propagate *Spartium* is by seed, which usually sets in abundance.

Spiraea

This large genus includes many useful garden shrubs. The 'Bridal Wreath' *Spiraea, S. × arguta,* is a lovely sight in late spring with the long arched branches covered in tight bunches of white flowers.

It is a shrub of medium stature reaching a final height of 6 ft (1.8 m). All spring-flowering *Spiraea* should be pruned after flowering. They can be propagated easily from summer cuttings.

Spiraea × bumalda 'Goldflame'

S. × bumalda 'Goldflame'

This is an attractive little *Spiraea*, well worth planting for the striking mixture of yellow-to-orange foliage, which is especially bright in the spring. As spring moves on to summer the leaves become a mixture of bronze and green. The round trusses of flower are a dull crimson and look quite strange against the golden foliage. Prune it hard, early in the spring, to encourage bright new growth. It is easy to propagate from summer cuttings.

S. 'Snowmound'

This exciting compact *Spiraea* is a native of the USA and puts on a great spring display with arched branches covered in massed bunches of white flowers. This excellent shrub will eventually grow to about 4 ft (1.2 m) under ideal conditions. Prune hard after flowering to encourage plenty of new, strong shoots. It is easy to root from summer cuttings.

Syringa (Lilac)

S. 'Charles Joly'

Today we have an anormous selection of lovely colours to choose from among the lilacs, including this excellent deep purple double-flowered variety. Fortunately the majority of lilacs are now propagated from cuttings, which eliminates the irritating problem of suckers. Plant in good rich soil and be sure to dead-head immediately they have stopped flowering. This is one shrub that will thrive on chalk.

S. × josiflexa 'Bellicent'

Here we have one of the excellent Canadian hybrids, which grows to a height of around 10 ft (3 m), producing large plumes of soft pink flowers in early summer.

Tamarix juniperina

S. microphylla 'Superba'

This is an excellent dwarf lilac that does not exceed 6 ft (1.8 m) in height. Deep rose pink sprays of flower cover this compact shrub early in the summer, and the flowers have an added bonus of being deliciously scented. Prune lightly after flowering to retain a compact shape. This is a moderately easy shrub to root from cuttings.

S. vulgaris 'Katherine Havemeyer'

This is one of the very best lilacs with enormous double plumes of lavender flowers fading in time to lilac pink.

Spiraea 'Snowmound'

S. vulgaris 'Mme. Lemoine'

There is something really exciting about white lilac, and this is certainly one of the best with large double flowers.

S. vulgaris 'Primrose'

We always look for the unusual in all our shrubs, and here is a break in colour with a true yellow single-flowered lilac.

Tamarix

This lovely shrub is sadly neglected; for many it is considered for seaside planting only where it will certainly thrive with roots growing into the sea. As a garden plant, however, *T. pentandra* is well worth planting for the light feathery foliage and glorious pink haze effect of the massed pink flowers that arrive late in the summer. It is essential to prune all *Tamarix* quite hard to keep a

147

Viburnum davidii

really compact shape. There is an earlier flowering species called *T. tetrandra* that will flower in early summer. To propagate, root from summer cuttings.

Viburnum

V. × bodnantense 'Dawn'

Many winter-flowering shrubs can be rather lacking in both size and colour of flower, but this one is certainly an exception. Planted against a

Viburnum × bodnantense 'Dawn'

good dark green background the naked branches are covered in a mass of deep pink scented flowers from autumn right through the winter. Fairly constant pruning is advisable, otherwise the shrubs can get rather leggy. Propagate from summer cuttings.

V. davidii

This is a really distinctive evergreen with leathery dark green leaves marked with deep lines. This is a shrub that is often planted as ground cover; in mass it forms a low round dome eventually achieving 5 ft (1.5 m) in height and 7 – 8 ft (2 – 2.4 m) in width. The dense green foliage will totally cover the ground suppressing any weeds. The small clustered heads of flower are really fairly unexciting but in autumn these are followed

by bunches of lovely brilliant blue berries. Ideally plant two or three plants together, as this will guarantee a good crop of berries. You often find male or female flowers on one plant which will not produce berries on its own. Propagate from late summer cuttings (not easy).

V. opulus

V. opulus is the guelder rose with the distinctive flat white flowers arriving in summer, followed in the autumn by a crop of brilliant red translucent berries resembling large red currants. At the same time the leaves give a brilliant display of autumn colour. *V. o.* 'Notcutts Variety' is a lovely selected form of this shrub with extra large flowers and red berries. There is a smaller form called *V.o.* 'Compactum' which will eventually grow to about 5 ft (1.5 m) as opposed to 'Notcutts Variety' which can be as tall as 12 ft (3.6 m). Also worth growing are the two yellow-berried forms *V. o.* 'Fructuluteo' and *V. o.* 'Xanthocarpum'. All root easily from cuttings.

V. plicatum 'Grandiflorum'

This is really a superb shrub giving a wonderful display of colour each spring. It is commonly called the Japanese Snowball Tree, a name that aptly describes the large white flowers shaped like a large ball. *V. plicatum* is an equally lovely shrub with a mass of rather smaller snowball like flowers. Both will root easily from cuttings.

V. plicatum 'Mariesii'

Every spring these shrubs put on a magnificent display of white lacecap flowers. The tiered habit of growth shows off the flowers to marvellous effect. It is a shrub that will eventually grow quite large, 9 – 10 ft (2.7 – 3 m) in height and equally wide. It is easy to root from summer cuttings.

V. plicatum 'Pink Beauty'

On this charming *Viburnum*, the florets flush to

Viburnum plicatum 'Pink Beauty'

various shades of pink as they age. It is quite compact and ideal for the smaller garden.

V. tinus 'Eve Price'

The new cultivars of *V. tinus* have made this one of the best and most colourful winter-flowering shrubs. 'Eve Price' has a compact habit, and is very free-flowering, starting the winter with a mass of deep pink tinted buds opening to pale pink flowers. It will grow in full sun, where it appears to be very happy. To keep a compact bush it is wise to clip the plants after flowering.

V. tinus 'Gwenllian'

This is perhaps not quite so hardy as 'Eve Price' but the flowers are really beautiful and large. The buds are deep red opening to a mixture of red, pink and white. The leaves are a fairly distinctive dark green. It is easy to root from summer cuttings.

Weigela

W. 'Bristol Ruby'

This is perhaps one of the easiest of all deciduous shrubs to grow. *W.* 'Bristol Ruby' has wine red flowers and bright green leaves giving a fine spring display of colour.

W. florida 'Foliis purpureis'

This is rather a sombre shrub with light purple leaves and flowers of matching colour. If carefully placed in the garden it can add an interesting colour contrast.

W. florida 'Variegata'

In this, one of the most effective of all variegated shrubs, the leaves are pale green edged with cream. The delicate pink flowers show up well against the light foliage. As with all *Weigela* prune well after the early summer flowers to keep a compact vigorous bush with plenty of new foliage.

W. 'looymansii aurea'

Here we have the gold-leaved member of this genus with pretty pink flowers. The leaves are rather delicate so plant in light shade to avoid sun scorch. All members of this genus root very easily from summer cuttings.

Yucca

Y. filamentosa is a shrub with a tropical look. It is not an easy plant to place in the garden, preferring a hot dry site where it is best planted in large clumps. It can also make an interesting shrub for pots or tubs. The flowers consist of a very dramatic tall spike up to 6 ft (1.8 m) high, covered in a mass of white bell-like flowers. Propagate by means of offshoots. *Y. filamentosa* 'Variegata' is a very attractive variegated form with green and silver leaves. Plant in a well-drained sheltered site.

Yucca filamentosa

Appendix

Shrubs of Special Interest Throughout the Year

Hibiscus
Hydrangea
Hypericum
Laurus nobilis
Lavandula augustifolia 'Hidcote'
   L. augustifolia 'Munstead'
Lippia citriodora
Myrtus communis
Phlomis fruticosa
Potentilla
Romneya × hybrida 'White Cloud'
Rosa
Rosmarinus officinalis 'Miss
   Jessop's Variety'
   R. officinalis 'Severn Sea'
Sorbaria arborea
Spartium junceum
Tamarix pentandra
Yucca filamentosa
   Y. filamentosa 'Variegata'

Winter-flowering and Foliage Shrubs

Arundinaria
Aucuba
Chimonanthus praecox
   'Grandiflorus'
Cornus alba 'Sibirica'
   C. mas
   C. stolonifera 'Flaviramea'
Elaeagnus 'Gilt Edge'
   E. 'Limelight'
   E. 'Maculata Aurea'
Erica carnea 'Alan Coates'
   E. carnea 'December Red'
   E. carnea 'King George'
   E. carnea 'Pink Spangles'
   E. carnea 'Springwood Pink'
   E. carnea 'Springwood White'
   E. carnea 'Vivellii'
   E. darleyensis 'Darley Dale'
   E. darleyensis 'George Rendall'
   E. darleyensis 'Silberschmelze'
Euonymus fortunei 'Emerald &
   Gold'
   E. fortunei 'Emerald Gaiety'
   E. japonicus 'Aureopictus'
Garrya elliptica
   G. elliptica 'James Roof'
Griselinia littoralis
Hamamelis

Hippophae rhamnoides
Ilex
Leucothoe fontanesiana
   'Rainbow'
Lonicera
Mahonia
Parrotia persica
Phormium tenax
   P. tenax 'Purpureum'
Pittosporum
Sarcococca confusa
Viburnum bodnantense 'Dawn'
   V. tinus 'Eve Price'
   V. tinus 'Gwenllian'

Autumn Colour (including berries and fruits

Acer palmatum 'Bloodgood'
   A. palmatum 'Dissectum'
   A. palmatum 'Trompenburg'
Amelanchier laevis
Arbutus unedo 'Rubra'
Aucuba
Azalea, deciduous
Azalea, Japanese evergreen
   varieties
   A. 'Hinodegiri'
   A. 'Palestrina'
Berberis ottawensis 'Superba'
   B. thunbergii atropurpurea
   B. thunbergii 'Kelleris'
Cornus alba 'Sibirica'
   C. stolonifera 'Flaviramea'
Cotinus coggygria
   C. coggygria 'Foliis Purpureis'
     ''Notcutt's Variety''
Cotoneaster 'Cornubia'
   C. dammeri
   C. 'Exburiensis'
   C. horizontalis
   C. horizontalis 'Variegatus'
   C. 'Hybridus Pendulus'
Elaeagnus 'Gilt Edge'
   E. 'Limelight'
   E. 'Maculata Aurea'
Enkianthus campanulatus
Fothergilla major
Hamamelis intermedia 'Jelena'
Hypericum inodorum 'Elstead'
Ilex aquifolium 'Argentea
   Marginata'

   I. 'Ferox Argentea'
   I. 'Golden Milkboy'
   I. 'Handsworth New Silver'
   I. 'J.C. van Tol'
   I. 'Pyramidalis Fructuluteo'
Leucothoe fontanesiana
   'Rainbow'
Pernettya mucronata 'Bell's
   Seedling'
   P. mucronata 'Cherry Ripe'
   P. mucronata 'Lilacina'
   P. mucronata 'Pink Pearl'
   P. mucronata 'White Pearl'
Pittosporum tenuifolium
   'Garnettii'
   P. tenuifolium 'Silver Queen'
   P. tenuifolium tenuifolium
   P. tenuifolium 'Tom Thumb'
   P. tenuifolium 'Warnham Gold'
Pyracantha 'Alexander Pendula'
   P. 'Mohave'
   P. 'Orange Charmer'
   P. 'Orange Glow'
   P. 'Soleil d'Or'
   P. 'Variegata'
Rhus typhina

Autumn-flowering and Foliage Shrubs

Camellia sasanqua
Ceanothus 'Autumnal Blue'
Elaeagnus ebbingei
Fatsia japonica

Ground Cover

Berberis thunbergii 'Little
   Favourite'
Calluna vulgaris 'Alba Plena'
   C. vulgaris 'Alportii'
   C. vulgaris 'County Wicklow'
   C. vulgaris 'Elsie Purell'
   C. vulgaris 'Gold Haze'
   C. vulgaris 'Golden feather'
   C. vulgaris 'H.E. Beale'
   C. vulgaris 'Peter Sparkes'
   C. vulgaris 'Serlei'
   C. vulgaris 'Sunset'
   C. vulgaris 'Tib'
Ceanothus 'Blue Mound'

Cornus canadensis
Cotoneaster dammeri
  C. horizontalis
  C. horizontalis 'Variegatus'
Cytisus kewensis
Daboecia cantabrica 'Alba'
  D. cantabrica 'Atropurpurea'
  D. cantabrica 'Bicolor'
Erica carnea 'Alan Coates'
  E. carnea 'December Red'
  E. carnea 'King George'
  E. carnea 'Pink Spangles'
  E. carnea 'Springwood Pink'
  E. carnea 'Springwood White'
  E. carnea 'Vivellii'
  E. cineria 'Atrosanguinea'
  E. cineria 'C.D. Eason'
  E. cineria 'Eden Valley'
  E. cineria 'Fiddlers Gold'
  E. cineria 'Tilford'
  E. darleyensis 'Darley Dale'
  E. darleyensis 'George Rendall'
  E. darleyensis 'Silberschmelze'
  E. vagans 'Lyonesse'
  E. vagans 'Mrs. D.F. Maxwell'
Euonymus fortunei 'Emerald & Gold'
  E. fortunei 'Emerald Gaiety'
Gaultheria shallon
Genista hispanica
  G. lydia
Halimiocistus ingwersenii
  H. wintonensis
Halimium lasianthum
Hebe 'Carl Teschner'
Hypericum calycinum
Lavandula augustifolia 'Hidcote'
  L. augustifolia 'Munstead'
Mahonia aquifolium
Pernettya mucronata 'Bell's Seedling'
  P. mucronata 'Cherry Ripe'

P. mucronata 'Lilacina'
P. mucronata 'Pink Pearl'
P. mucronata 'White Pearl'
Potentilla 'Longacre'
Prunus laurocerasus 'Otto Luyken'
  P. laurocerasus 'Zabeliana'
Rhododendron, dwarf types
  R. 'Carmen'
  R. 'Creeping Jenny'
  R. impeditum
  R. 'Pink Drift'
Rosa 'Nozomi'
  R. rugosa 'Max Graf'
Viburnum davidii

Shrubs for Screens or Hedges

Berberis candidula
  B. darwinii
  B. ottawensis 'Superba'
  B. 'Stapehill'
  B. stenophylla
  B. verruculosa
Cotoneaster 'Cornubia'
  C. 'Exburiensis'
Elaeagnus ebbingei
Escallonia
Griselinia littoralis
Hippophae rhamnoides
Ilex
Laurus nobilis
  L. nitida 'Baggeson's Gold'
Osmanthus delavayi
Osmarea burkwoodii
Philadelphus 'Belle Etoile'
  P. coronarius
  P. coronarius 'Aureus'
  P. 'Virginal'
Pittosporum tenuifolium 'Garnettii'

P. tenuifolium 'Silver Queen'
P. tenuifolium tenuifolium
P. tenuifolium 'Warnham Gold'
Prunus cerasifera 'Pissardii'
  P. laurocerasus
  P. laurocerasus 'Otto Luyken'
  P. laurocerasus 'Zabeliana'
  P. lusitanica
Pyracantha
Rhododendron, large types
Syringa 'Charles Joly'
Viburnum tinus 'Eve Price'
  V. tinus 'Gwenllian'

Shrubs for Shade

Arundinaria
Aucuba
Azalea, Japanese evergreen varieties
Camellia
Gaultheria shallon
Hydrangea
Hypericum calycinum
Pernettya
Pieris
Rhododendron, dwarf types
Rhododendron, medium types
Rhododendron, large types
Skimmia

Plants with Aromatic Foliage

Laurus nobilis
Lippia citriodora
Myrtus communis
Ribes sanguineum
Rosmarinus officinalis 'Miss Jessop's Variety'
  R. officinalis 'Severn Sea'
  Ruta 'Jackman's Blue'

Index of Latin Names

Figures in **bold** refer to page numbers of colour illustrations.

General Index